365

Days of

Prophetic Devotion

A Year of Daily Transformation

Allison Velazquez

Copyright © 2024, Allison Velazquez

Published by Johnson Tribe Publishing, LLC, Atlanta, GA

All rights reserved, including the expressed right to reproduce this book or portions thereof in any form whatsoever, whether now known or hereinafter developed. This book may not be copied or reproduced without the expressed written permission of the author or publisher. The author is also available for speaking engagements and may be contacted at allisonmfvelazquez1993@gmail.com

Manufactured in the United States of America.

ISBN: 979-8-9909350-6-8

First Edition USA $24.99

*All Scripture references in this book are from the Holy Bible, utilizing three versions: King James Version (KJV), New International Version (NIV), and the New Revised Standard Version Updated Edition (NRSVUE).

DEDICATION

I dedicate this book to all my brothers and sisters in Christ Jesus. When you open this prophetic devotional, I pray that the holy spirit speaks to you and the Lord's presence saturates you. Thank you to all who stood by me and prayed for me. Thank you to my Fatherly in Heaven, who gave me this vision to write this book. I know this prophetic devotional is going to change many lives. May the Lord bless you and keep you in Jesus' name. Thank you to my husband, who helped me push through and encouraged me to write this book, and to my beautiful children, Christian and Sofia. I love you all so much! You all are indeed a blessing from God.

INTRODUCTION

I've been working on this 365-day devotional since 2022. when God gave me the vision to write a 356-day devotional book, I began to write as the holy spirit spoke to me. I want to thank God for not letting me give up. Many of you know me from social media platforms such as YouTube, Facebook, Instagram, etc., and thank you for your prayers. God himself has truly anointed this book. On each page, you will find a word from the Lord. No matter where you are walking with the Lord, know he is with you and will never leave or forsake you. I pray that this book changes your life and transforms you into the woman or man of God you are called to be. Jesus loves you!

Table of Contents

Dedication iii
Introduction iv
January 1st 1
January 2nd 3
January 3rd 4
January 4th 5
January 5th 7
January 6th 8
January 7th 9
January 8th 10
January 9th 11
January 10th 12
January 11th 13
January 12th 14
January 13th 15
January 14th 16
January 15th 17
January 16th 18
January 17th 19
January 18th 20
January 19th 21
January 20th 22
January 21st 24
January 22nd 25

January 23rd 26
January 24th 28
January 25th 29
January 26th 30
January 27th 31
January 28th 32
January 29th 33
January 30th 34
February 1st 36
February 2nd 37
February 3rd 38
February 4th 39
February 5th 40
February 6th 42
February 7th 43
February 8th 44
February 9th 45
February 10th 47
February 11th 48
February 12th 49
February 13th 50
February 14th 51
February 15th 53
February 16th 55
February 17th 56
February 18th 57
February 19th 58

February 20th 59
February 21st 60
February 22nd 61
February 23rd 62
February 24th 63
February 25th 64
February 26th 65
February 27th 66
February 28th 67
February 29th 68
March 1st 69
March 2nd 71
March 3rd 72
March 4th 73
March 5th 74
March 6th 75
March 7th 76
March 8th 77
March 9th 78
March 10th 79
March 11th 80
March 12th 81
March 13th 82
March 14th 83
March 15th 84
March 16th 85
March 17th 86

March 18th	88
March 19th	89
March 20th	90
March 21st	91
March 22nd	92
March 23rd	93
March 24th	94
March 25th	95
March 26th	96
March 27th	97
March 28th	98
March 29th	99
March 30th	100
March 31st	101
April 1st	102
April 2nd	103
April 3rd	104
April 4th	105
April 5th	106
April 6th	107
April 7th	108
April 8th	109
April 9th	110
April 10th	111
April 11th	112
April 12th	114
April 13th	115

April 14th 117
April 15th 119
April 16th 120
April 17th 121
April 18th 122
April 19th 123
April 20th 124
April 21st 125
April 22nd 127
April 23rd 128
April 24th 129
April 25th 130
April 26th 131
April 27th 132
April 28th 133
April 29th 134
April 30th 135
May 1st 136
May 2nd 137
May 3rd 138
May 4th 139
May 5th 140
May 6th 141
May 7th 142
May 8th 143
May 9th 144
May 10th 145

May 11th	146
May 12th	147
May 13th	148
May 14th	149
May 15th	150
May 16th	151
May 17th	152
May 18th	154
May 19th	155
May 20th	156
May 21st	157
May 22nd	159
May 23rd	160
May 24th	161
May 25th	162
May 26th	163
May 27th	164
May 28th	166
May 29th	167
May 30th	168
May 31st	169
June 1st	170
June 2nd	171
June 3rd	172
June 4th	173
June 5th	174
June 6th	175

June 7th	176
June 8th	177
June 9th	178
June 10th	179
June 11th	180
June 12th	181
June 13th	182
June 14th	184
June 15th	185
June 16th	186
June 17th	187
June 18th	188
June 19th	189
June 20th	190
June 21st	191
June 22nd	192
June 23rd	193
June 24th	194
June 25th	195
June 26th	196
June 27th	197
June 28th	198
June 29th	199
June 30th	200
July 1st	201
July 2nd	202
July 3rd	203

July 4th	205
July 5th	206
July 6th	207
July 7th	208
July 8th	209
July 9th	211
July 10th	212
July 11th	213
July 12th	214
July 13th	215
July 14th	216
July 15th	217
July 16th	218
July 17th	219
July 18th	220
July 19th	221
July 20th	222
July 21st	223
July 22nd	224
July 23rd	225
July 24th	226
July 25th	227
July 26th	228
July 27th	229
July 28th	230
July 29th	231
July 30th	232

July 31st 233
August 1st 234
August 2nd 236
August 3rd 238
August 4th 239
August 5th 240
August 6th 241
August 7th 242
August 8th 244
August 9th 245
August 10th 246
August 11th 247
August 12th 248
August 13th 249
August 14th 250
August 15th 251
August 16th 252
August 17th 253
August 18th 254
August 19th 255
August 20th 256
August 21st 257
August 22nd 258
August 23rd 259
August 24th 261
August 25th 262
August 26th 263

August 27th	264
August 28th	265
August 29th	266
August 30th	267
August 31st	269
September 1st	270
September 2nd	271
September 3rd	272
September 4th	273
September 5th	274
September 6th	275
September 7th	276
September 8th	278
September 9th	279
September 10th	280
September 11th	281
September 12th	284
September 13th	285
September 14th	287
September 15th	288
September 16th	289
September 17th	290
September 18th	291
September 19th	292
September 20th	293
September 21st	295
September 22nd	296

September 23rd 298
September 24th 299
September 25th 300
September 26th 301
September 27th 302
September 28th 303
September 29th 304
September 30th 305
October 1st 306
October 2nd 307
October 3rd 308
October 4th 309
October 5th 310
October 6th 311
October 7th 312
October 8th 313
October 9th 315
October 10th 316
October 11th 317
October 12th 318
October 13th 319
October 14th 320
October 15th 321
October 16th 322
October 17th 323
October 18th 324
October 19th 325

October 20th	326
October 21st	327
October 22nd	328
October 23rd	329
October 24th	330
October 25th	331
October 26th	332
October 27th	333
October 28th	334
October 29th	335
October 30th	336
October 31st	337
November 1st	338
November 2nd	340
November 3rd	341
November 4th	342
November 5th	343
November 6th	345
November 7th	346
November 8th	347
November 9th	348
November 10th	349
November 11th	350
November 12th	351
November 13th	352
November 14th	353
November 15th	354

November 16th 355
November 17th 356
November 18th 357
November 19th 358
November 20th 359
November 21st 361
November 22nd 362
November 23rd 363
November 24th 365
November 25th 366
November 26th 367
November 27th 368
November 28th 369
November 29th 370
November 30th 371
December 1st 372
December 2nd 373
December 3rd 375
December 4th 376
December 5th 377
December 6th 378
December 7th 379
December 8th 380
December 9th 381
December 10th 382
December 11th 383
December 12th 384

December 13th 385
December 14th 386
December 15th 387
December 16th 388
December 17th 389
December 18th 390
December 19th 391
December 20th 392
December 21st 393
December 22nd 394
December 23rd 395
December 24th 396
December 25th 397
December 26th 398
December 27th 399
December 28th 400
December 29th 401
December 30th 403
December 31st 404
About the Author 405

JANUARY 1ST

Surrender

Exodus 20:3-6

³ "You shall have no other gods before[a] me. ⁴ "You shall not make for yourself an image in the form of anything in heaven above or on the earth beneath or in the waters below. ⁵ You shall not bow down to them or worship them; for I, the Lord your God, am a jealous God, punishing the children for the sin of the parents to the third and fourth generation of those who hate me, ⁶ but showing love to a thousand generations of those who love me and keep my commandments.

Leviticus 19:4

⁴ Do not turn to idols or make metal gods for yourselves. I am the Lord your God.

The Father is saying to surrender your whole being to me, have no room for doubt or unbelief, and believe that all things are possible with me. This message is for those who think and have faith in God alone. Ask the Holy Spirit to reveal and search your heart and surrender anything that is not of me, saith the Lord, for I am always working and moving. I've extended my grace upon you to surrender the thing you're struggling with today and release it into my hands. You've idealized people unintentionally for so long, and I know you're ready for a fresh start. Today, repent of idolizing people or things in your life. Let go, and let me go to work. It's time to grow spiritually with me as I guide you and lead you in all truth. I will never lead you astray, nor will I fail you. I need you to forgive yourself for all that happened to you in your past. You are a new creation in Christ Jesus. I know you have made some bad decisions, but that wrong decision does not define you. I do sayeth the Lord you shall have no other gods before me. "You shall not make yourself an idol or likeness of what is in heaven above, on the earth beneath, or in the water under the earth. You shall not worship them or serve them, for I, the Lord your God, am a jealous God, visiting the iniquity of the fathers on the children, on the third and the fourth generations of those who hate me, but showing loving kindness to thousands, to those who love me and keep my commandments.

JANUARY 2ᴺᴰ

Peace

John 14:27

Peace I leave with you; my peace I give you. I do not give to you as the world gives. Do not let your hearts be troubled, and do not be afraid.

John 15:16

You did not choose me, but I chose you and appointed you so that you might go and bear fruit - fruit that will last–and so that whatever you ask in my name the Father will give you.

The Father is saying that you should not let your heart be troubled by the things happening around you. Stay focused on Him and what He has spoken to and about you. Do not be afraid. Know that God will give you the strength you need in everything, not just some things. He will be with you on this journey, and you will never be alone. He has given you the Holy Spirit, your helper, to support you in all you do. When you feel alone, take authority over the spirit of loneliness and cast it away. The devil wants you to believe you are alone, but he is always a liar and a thief. Remember, God has chosen and appointed you, not men. Since you are chosen by God, you have the authority to live a life of faith that honors Him and produces good works.

JANUARY 3ᴿᴰ

Listen

John 10:27

My sheep listen to my voice; I know them, and they follow me.

The Father is saying that as a child of God, you should listen for and recognize His voice because He will feed, guide, and protect you. God is your shepherd and will guide and direct you if you ask the Holy Spirit to quiet other voices and increase His voice so that you can hear and follow him. Through His word, God assures you that you can always bring Him your concerns and ask Him anything. There's no need to hide anything from Him because you are the chosen one, and if you will listen, He will enable you to hear the truth. If you follow Him, there is no need to fear tomorrow, for He will give you eternal life, a future, and hope.

JANUARY 4ᵀᴴ

The Power of Humility and Honor

Isaiah 25:11

And He will spread out His hands in their midst. As a swimmer reaches out to swim, And He will bring down their pride. Together with the trickery of their hands.

1 Samuel 2:30

Therefore the Lord, the God of Israel, declares: 'I promised that your house and the house of your father should go in and out before me forever,' but now the Lord declares: 'Far be it from me, for those who honor me I will honor, and those who despise me shall be lightly esteemed.

The Father is saying in Isaiah 25:11 we see a powerful image of God stretching out His hands, like a swimmer pushing through water, to bring down the pride of those who stand against Him. This passage reminds us that no amount of pride or deceit can stand before God's sovereign power. As water yields to a swimmer's hands, so will the proud be brought low by God's mighty hand. God does not tolerate pride, especially when it is coupled with deceit and manipulation.

1 Samuel 2:30 shows us God's response to both honor and dishonor. God had promised Eli's house a perpetual priesthood, but because they dishonored Him, God withdrew that promise. The principle here is clear: God honors those who honor Him, but those who despise Him will be humbled.

These scriptures call us to a life of humility and honor before God. Pride and self-reliance are dangerous traps that lead to downfall, but humility opens the door to God's favor. When we honor God in our thoughts, actions, and words, we position ourselves to receive His honor in return. It is a reminder that God is not only just but also deeply personal in how He responds to our attitudes and behaviors.

Let us strive to honor God in all we do, trusting that He will bring down the strongholds of pride in our lives and elevate us according to His perfect will.

JANUARY 5TH

Trust in the Shepherd

Psalm 23:1-3;

The Lord is my shepherd; I lack nothing. He makes me lie down in green pastures; he leads me beside quiet waters, and he refreshes my soul. He guides me along the right paths for his name's sake.

Ezekiel 12:25;

But I, the Lord, will speak what I will, and it shall be fulfilled without delay. For in your days, you rebellious people, I will fulfill whatever I say, declares the Sovereign Lord.'

The Father is saying that when we face brutal battles or life feels overwhelming, we never have to run away in fear because the Lord is our Shepherd, and we shall fear no evil. Knowing that God is our Shepherd means understanding that we will lack nothing we need. He provides for every need and fulfills every desire in our hearts.

God reminds us not to fear evil because He is always with us, no matter where we go. If He has spoken a promise, we can trust it will pass. Even if our faith is as small as a mustard seed, God faithfully fulfills His word.

The Lord assures us it will be fulfilled without delay when He speaks. For those who hope in Him alone, His promises will come to pass. Even amid rebellion or doubt, God declares He will fulfill what He has spoken.

So, take heart and trust in the Shepherd. He is with you, guiding, providing, and bringing His promises to your life.

JANUARY 6ᵀᴴ

Joy in the Journey

> Psalm 37:23

The Lord makes firm the steps of the one who delights in him;

> Colossians 1:10

¹⁰ So that you may live a life worthy of the Lord and please him in every way: bearing fruit in every good work, growing in the knowledge of God.

So that you may live a life worthy of the Lord and please him in every way: bearing fruit in every good work, growing in the knowledge of God,

The Father is saying, "Find joy in this journey with Me as you walk into My will and your purpose." Remember, the Lord orders your steps and delights in how you follow Him. Trust in Me with all your heart in every area of your life. You've prayed and asked for My will to be done, and My will for your life is that you prosper in everything you do.

To walk in a manner worthy of the Lord means to be fully pleasing to Him, bearing fruit in every good work and growing in the knowledge of God. The goal is not perfection but progression and progress. Together, we will bear much fruit and accomplish one goal at a time.

There is no need to hurry; rest easy in My presence, knowing that I am your Father who provides and gives you all you need. Every perfect gift comes from above, My beloved. Trust in this journey, for I am with you every step.

JANUARY 7TH

Fasting with Purpose

Matthew 6:5-6

And when you pray, do not be like the hypocrites, for they love to pray, standing in the synagogues and on the street corners to be seen by others. Truly, I tell you, they have received their reward in full. **6** But when you pray, go into your room, close the door, and pray to your Father, who is unseen. Then your Father, who sees what is done in secret, will reward you.

Matthew 6:17-19

But when you fast, put oil on your head and wash your face, 18 so that it will not be obvious to others that you are fasting, but only to your Father, who is unseen; and your Father, who sees what is done in secret, will reward you.

The Father is saying, "When you fast, anoint your head with oil and wash your face. In doing this, you put aside your fleshly desires and seek My perfect will for your life." Instead of giving in to weakness or complaining, turn your focus to praise and worship. Bow down before Me and sing praises to My holy name, and watch every evil force flee from you in Jesus' name. Shift your attention from the distractions around you and refocus on Me. The enemy thrives on distractions, so ask My Holy Spirit for discernment to recognize and resist his tactics. And when you pray, don't be like the hypocrites who love to pray in public just to be seen. Not you, beloved—I see you. Your flesh may be weak, but the Spirit of the living God dwells within you. Trust in My strength, and let your fasting and prayers draw you closer to My will.

JANUARY 8th

Acting in Faith

Isaiah 51:16

I have put my words in your mouth
and covered you with the shadow of my hand—
I who set the heavens in place,
who laid the foundations of the earth,
and who say to Zion, 'You are my people.'"

Deuteronomy 31:8

The Lord himself goes before you and will be with you; he will never leave you nor forsake you. Do not be afraid; do not be discouraged."

The Father is saying, when you do anything in My name, do it by faith. My name is above every other, holding all power and authority in heaven and on earth. When you speak the name of Jesus, devils must bow, and sickness is healed. Whether eating, drinking, or feeling led by the Holy Spirit to pray for someone, do it with faith without fear.

If you prophesy, do it by faith, with confidence. Do not fear, for I am the Lord your God. I will uphold you with My righteous right hand—you will not fall. When you speak, I will put the words in your mouth. Again, I say, do not be afraid. Don't worry about anything; pray about everything until something happens.

I am always speaking to you. Don't be deceived by the enemy any longer; know I am with you. I go before, behind, and around you—you are never alone. Trust in My presence and act boldly in My name, knowing that I am with you every step of the way.

JANUARY 9TH

A Living Sacrifice

Psalm 119:105

Your word is a lamp for my feet, a light on my path.

Romans 12:1

Therefore, I urge you, brothers and sisters, in view of God's mercy, to offer your bodies as a living sacrifice, holy and pleasing to God—this is your true and proper worship.

1 Corinthians 6:19-20

Do you not know that your bodies are temples of the Holy Spirit, who is in you, whom you have received from God? You are not your own; [20,] you were bought at a price. Therefore, honor God with your bodies.

The Father is saying, therefore, I urge you, brothers and sisters, in light of God's mercy, to offer your bodies as a living sacrifice, holy and pleasing to God. This is your true and proper worship. I have called you to be holy because I am holy. I have removed certain things from your life that no longer served you, and now that you have released them to Me, I can give you what you truly need. I will place it in your hands, and what I give you will be yours—no one can take it away.

I know what is best for you, for I created you. Do you not know that your body is a temple of the Holy Spirit within you, whom you received from God? You are not your own; you were bought with a price. So, glorify God in your body, for it is My dwelling place. Trust in My wisdom and let your life be a sacrifice dedicated to My purpose and glory.

JANUARY 10TH

Utter Devotion

> **1 Kings 8:61**
>
> And may your hearts be fully committed to the Lord our God, to live by his decrees and obey his commands, as at this time."

> **Colossians 4:2**
>
> Devote yourselves to prayer, being watchful and thankful.

The Father is saying to be utterly devoted to Me. Let your heart be wholly committed to the Lord our God, to walk in His statutes and keep His commandments, starting today. I am faithful in keeping my promises and have never let you down. Have I ever failed you? God is not a man that He should lie or change His mind. What He has said, He will do. What He has spoken, He will fulfill. My promises are yes and amen.

Be mindful to pray for others. As your Father, I know what you need and your heart's desires. But others also need to know Me; when they encounter Me through you, they will experience true love. You are a reflection of Me, My beloved. My love for you is unshakable and cannot be taken away, in Jesus' name.

JANUARY 11ᵀᴴ

Rest in His Perfect Way

Psalm 18:20

The Lord has dealt with me according to my righteousness;

according to the cleanness of my hands, he has rewarded me.

Matthew 11:28-30

"Come to me, all you who are weary and burdened, and I will give you rest. ²⁹ Take my yoke upon you and learn from me, for I am gentle and humble in heart, and you will find rest for your souls. ³⁰ For my yoke is easy, and my burden is light."

The Father is saying that for God, His ways are perfect. The word of the Lord is proven and true. He is a shield to all who trust in Him. My way is excellent, and My word is truth. Everything you want and need, you will find in Me.

My way may not always be easy, but take My yoke upon you—it is easy, and My burden is light. When you feel weary and burdened, come to Me, and you will find rest for your soul. My yoke is light because it is the yoke of repentance, faith, and a commitment to follow Me. Trust in My perfect way, and you will find peace and rest in My presence.

JANUARY 12ᵀᴴ

Renewed Strength in Faith

Isaiah 40:31

but those who hope in the Lord
will renew their strength.
They will soar on wings like eagles;
they will run and not grow weary,
they will walk and not be faint.

Isaiah 41:13

For I am the Lord your God
who takes hold of your right hand
and says to you, Do not fear;
I will help you.

The Father is saying, draw near to Me in faith, and I will draw near to you. I will renew your strength. You will soar on wings like eagles; you will run and not grow weary; you will walk and not faint, even when you feel weak and unable to go on. Remember, when you are weak, you are strong because you rely on Me for your help.

You will feel My righteous hand strengthening you as you lean on Me. You will no longer tire quickly, for I, the Lord, sustain and consecrate you. You will not be moved or shaken. It is My foundation that plants you and upholds you, in Jesus' name. Trust in My strength, and find rest and renewal in My presence.

JANUARY 13TH

Faith and Breakthrough

Matthew 16:8

Aware of their discussion, Jesus asked, "You of little faith, why are you talking among yourselves about having no bread?

Luke 12:7

Indeed, the very hairs of your head are all numbered. Don't be afraid; you are worth more than many sparrows.

The Father is saying, Oh, you of little faith, is anything impossible for Me? Declares the Lord. There is nothing beyond My power. It is through faith that you will receive your breakthrough. Through faith, you will find complete freedom, healing, and restoration. I have never failed you, have I?

Ask My Holy Spirit to increase your faith, and My power will fall fresh upon you. I am working on your behalf every day. Remember, the very hairs on your head are all numbered. Do not be afraid; you are worth more than many sparrows. Trust in My boundless power and let your faith lead you to the miracles I have in store.

JANUARY 14TH

Overcoming Doubt

James 1:17-18

¹⁷ Every good and perfect gift is from above, coming down from the Father of the heavenly lights, who does not change like shifting shadows. ¹⁸ He chose to give us birth through the word of truth, that we might be a kind of first fruits of all he created.

Deuteronomy 28:8

The Lord will send a blessing on your barns and on everything you put your hand to. The Lord your God will bless you in the land he is giving you.

The Father is saying when you begin to doubt, you limit what you can accomplish in and through you. Do not doubt what I have spoken to you. Instead, seek My face and ask My Holy Spirit to remove anything that is not of Me. Shake off every doubt and dispel all confusion. Cast it back to the abyss in Jesus' name.

You have hope and a future in Me. You have direct access to Me, your heavenly Father. I am your Abba Father, and you are a chosen people, a royal priesthood, a holy nation, and God's special possession. You are called to declare the praises of Him, who has brought you out of darkness and into His wonderful light. Trust in this truth and let your faith shine brightly.

JANUARY 15TH

Expecting Abundant Blessings

James 1:17-18

¹⁷ Every good and perfect gift is from above, coming down from the Father of the heavenly lights, who does not change like shifting shadows. ¹⁸ He chose to give us birth through the word of truth, that we might be a kind of first fruits of all he created.

Deuteronomy 28:8

The Lord will send a blessing on your barns and on everything you put your hand to. The Lord your God will bless you in the land he is giving you.

The Father is saying, you are about to be amazed by the blessings that are about to touch down from heaven. Every perfect gift comes from above, from the Father of the heavenly lights, who remains constant and unchanging. Everything you have been asking for is on its way to you.

That job you have been praying for, the family member you have been lifting in prayer, and the marriage you fear might never be restored—each of these will be healed and restored in the mighty name of Jesus. Your financial breakthrough is coming, just as you have believed by faith.

If you fully obey the Lord your God and carefully follow all His commands, He will set you above all the nations on earth. You will be blessed in the city and blessed in the country. Trust in these promises, and prepare to receive His abundant blessings in store for you.

JANUARY 16ᵀᴴ

Trusting the Impossibility

> **1 Corinthians 10:31**

¹ So whether you eat or drink or whatever you do, do it all for the glory of God.

> **Jeremiah 23:24**

Who can hide in secret places
so that I cannot see them?"
declares the Lord.
"Do not I fill heaven and earth?"
declares the Lord.

The Father is saying that nothing is impossible for Me. When you ask by faith, you will receive all you ask for, according to My will. Many of My children feel discouraged when they don't receive what they ask for. But ask yourself: Is it My will, and will it glorify Me? Bring every request to My Holy Spirit for guidance.

Whether you eat or drink, or whatever you do, do it all for the glory of God. Remember, I am always with you. When you feel overwhelmed or uncertain, whisper My name, Jesus, and I will be right there with you.

Can a person hide so that I do not see them? Declares the Lord. Do I not fill the heavens and the earth? Declares the Lord. Trust that I am with you every moment, and find peace in My presence.

JANUARY 17ᵀᴴ

The One Voice That Matters

Luke 10:42

but few things are needed—or indeed only one.[a] Mary has chosen what is better, and it will not be taken away from her."

Hebrews 8:10

This is the covenant I will establish with the people of Israel
after that time, declares the Lord.
I will put my laws in their minds
and write them on their hearts.
I will be their God,
and they will be my people.

The Father is saying that many voices clamor for your attention, but only one resides with you and through you, and that is Mine, declares the Lord. Remember that spending time with Me in the secret place truly matters amid the many distractions around you.

Only a few things are needed, or rather, only one. Mary has chosen what is better, which will not be taken away from her. Know that you are in the right place at the right time. If you have been questioning this, I confirm that you are exactly where you should be. Choosing what is better means securing what cannot be taken away. Trust in this and find peace in My presence.

JANUARY 18th

Rejoice Through the Trials

Isaiah 43:2

When you pass through the waters, I will be with you, and when you pass through the rivers, they will not sweep over you. When you walk through the fire, you will not be burned; the flames will not set you ablaze.

2 Chronicles 20:15

He said: "Listen, King Jehoshaphat and all who live in Judah and Jerusalem! This is what the Lord says to you: 'Do not be afraid or discouraged because of this vast army. For the battle is not yours, but God's.

The Father is saying, "Fix your crown, daughter of Zion." You will face many trials, tests, and even persecutions, but I say to you, rejoice. Your suffering will not be in vain. When you walk through the fire, you will not be burned; the flames will not set you ablaze. No harm will come near you.

Though it may feel like this battle is impossible, remember that the battle is not yours—it is the Lord's. Since the battle is Mine, victory has already been secured in every area of your life. Take heart and trust that My will for your life is perfect. Rejoice in the certainty of My victory and the fulfillment of My promises.

JANUARY 19th

Guarding Your Thoughts

2 Corinthians 10:5

We demolish arguments and every pretension that sets itself up against the knowledge of God, and we take captive every thought to make it obedient to Christ.

John 1:1

In the beginning was the Word, and the Word was with God, and the Word was God.

The Father is saying you have many thoughts in your mind, but not all of them are from Me. Some thoughts may come from the enemy. When this happens, ask My Holy Spirit to take every thought captive and make it obedient to Christ Jesus.

Pray this: "Holy Spirit, I thank You for my life and my mind, which is whole and covered by the blood of Jesus. May Your presence control my mindset and set me apart in Jesus' name. I cast down every imagination and every high thing that exalts itself against the knowledge of God, bringing every thought into captivity to the obedience of Christ Jesus."

Trust that My Spirit will guide your thoughts and protect your mind.

JANUARY 20TH

Victory in Christ

Deuteronomy 28:7

The Lord will grant that the enemies who rise up against you will be defeated before you. They will come at you from one direction but flee from you in seven.

Mark 4:35-41

That day, when evening came, he said to his disciples, "Let us go over to the other side." ³⁶ Leaving the crowd behind, they took him along, just as he was, in the boat. There were also other boats with him. ³⁷ A furious squall came up, and the waves broke over the boat so that it was nearly swamped. ³⁸ Jesus was in the stern, sleeping on a cushion. The disciples woke him and said to him, "Teacher, don't you care if we drown?"

³⁹ He got up, rebuked the wind, and said to the waves, "Quiet! Be still!" Then, the wind died down, and it was completely calm.

⁴⁰ He said to his disciples, "Why are you so afraid? Do you still have no faith?"

⁴¹ They were terrified and asked each other, "Who is this? Even the wind and the waves obey him!"

The Father is saying when defeat tries to knock you down, remind the enemy that he has already been defeated. Victory has been secured in Christ Jesus. The Lord will cause your enemies who rise against you to be struck down before your eyes. They will come at you one way and flee from you seven ways.

When you feel the enemy's attacks trying to steal your peace and joy, command him to return to the abyss. Run to the secret place and seek Me above all else. As you spend time with Me, you will see the enemy flee seven ways in Jesus' name. Remember, there is no devil or demon beyond My power. I hold all authority, and every demon trembles before Me.

Who is this, that even the wind and sea obey Him? Oh, hallelujah, this is the good news! Trust in My power and watch as victory unfolds in your life.

JANUARY 21ST

Embracing the Father's Blessings

Isaiah 43:4

Since you are precious and honored in my sight, and because I love you, I will give people in exchange for you, nations in exchange for your life.

James 1:7

That person should not expect to receive anything from the Lord.

Genesis 3:13-14

Then the Lord God said to the woman, "What is this you have done?" The woman said, "The serpent deceived me, and I ate." 14 So the Lord God said to the serpent, "Because you have done this, "Cursed are you above all livestock and all wild animals! You will crawl on your belly, and you will eat dust all the days of your life.

The Father is saying, receive countless blessings upon you and your family. Never feel unworthy of the good things I have prepared for you. When you start to doubt your worthiness, cast that lie back into the abyss. Take authority over every diabolical force and bind it in the name of Jesus.

You are precious and honored in My eyes, and I love you deeply. Ask My Holy Spirit to bestow upon you the blessing of Abraham. I am preparing to pour out My blessings upon you, My beloved. Open your heart and receive all the Father has for you in Jesus' name.

JANUARY 22ND

Assurance in the Storm

2 Corinthians 10:4

The weapons we fight with are not the weapons of the world. On the contrary, they have divine power to demolish strongholds.

John 15:5

"I am the vine; you are the branches. If you remain in me and I in you, you will bear much fruit; apart from me, you can do nothing.

The Father is saying you may find that others do not understand the intensity of the attacks you face. Their comprehension may fall short. Yet, " I see and hear you, says the Lord. I know the dysfunction, confusion, and distractions the enemy brings into your life.

The devil often influences people without their awareness, using them and places and things to create obstacles. Sometimes, even habits can distract you. But take heart—my beloved child, I see and hear you. You are not alone in any storm, battle, or situation. The battles you face are not yours alone; they are Mine, declares the Lord.

I will give you the grace to overcome whether you encounter warfare, trials, or temptations. Remember, the weapons of our warfare are not of the flesh but are divinely powerful for tearing down strongholds. You can face anything with Me, but without Me, you cannot. Trust in My strength and presence, and know we will conquer all together.

JANUARY 23ᴿᴰ

Breaking Down Barriers

Mark 7:24-30

Jesus left that place and went to the vicinity of Tyre.[a] He entered a house and did not want anyone to know it, yet he could not keep his presence secret. ²⁵ In fact, as soon as she heard about him, a woman whose little daughter was possessed by an impure spirit came and fell at his feet. ²⁶ The woman was a Greek, born in Syrian Phoenicia. She begged Jesus to drive the demon out of her daughter. ²⁷ "First, let the children eat all they want," he told her, "for it is not right to take the children's bread and toss it to the dogs." ²⁸ "Lord," she replied, "even the dogs under the table eat the children's crumbs." ²⁹ Then he told her, "For such a reply, you may go; the demon has left your daughter." ³⁰ She went home and found her child lying on the bed, and the demon gone.

2 Corinthians 10:4-6

⁴ The weapons we fight with are not the weapons of the world. On the contrary, they have divine power to demolish strongholds.⁵ We demolish arguments and every pretension that sets itself up against the knowledge of God, and we take captive every thought to make it obedient to Christ. ⁶ And we will be ready to punish every act of disobedience once your obedience is complete.

The Father is saying, allow Me to dismantle every barrier in your life, including the strongholds you've built over time from past experiences. I am here to tear down every obstacle and stronghold in your way. Ask My Holy Spirit to remove every stronghold of fear and anxiety in the name of Jesus.

I know you intimately; I formed you with purpose. The enemy often uses fear as a tactic to hinder you. Remember, the battle is in your mind. Let Me set you free from these mental barriers.

Pray this prayer now: "Holy Spirit, thank You for making me whole in body, soul, and mind. I repent of all my sins and ask for Your forgiveness. Lord Jesus, break down every barrier the enemy has placed on my mind. Align my life with Your Word, which is truth, and let that truth set me free. I pray that every stronghold be restored to the abyss in Jesus' name. I am freed from every barrier and stronghold the enemy has had on my mind. I will praise and worship You with thanksgiving, knowing that whom the Son sets free is free indeed."

Rejoice and give thanks, for you are liberated from every stronghold that has bound you.

JANUARY 24ᵀᴴ

This Too Shall Pass

> 2 Corinthians 4:17-18

For our light and momentary troubles are achieving for us an eternal glory that far outweighs them all. ¹⁸ So we fix our eyes not on what is seen, but on what is unseen since what is seen is temporary, but what is unseen is eternal.

The Father is saying: "This too shall pass." Though enduring much suffering, remember that your pain will not be in vain. It is understandable to feel that you cannot continue another day because of the suffering you face, for My name's sake. Do not be swayed by your feelings or emotions. Instead, ask My Holy Spirit to help stabilize your emotions, bringing you the needed stability and balance. I am the God of order and here to provide that balance.

Our light and temporary affliction is working for us an eternal weight of glory. We are called to look beyond the visible and focus on the unseen. The things we see are temporary, but the things we do not see are eternal. Hold on to this truth and let it guide you through your struggles.

JANUARY 25ᵀᴴ

Return to Your First Love

Mark 10:9

⁹ Therefore what God has joined together, let no one separate."

Isaiah 54:17

no weapon forged against you will prevail,
And you will refute every tongue that accuses you.
This is the heritage of the servants of the Lord,
And this is their vindication from me,"

Declares the Lord.

The Father is saying you should return to your first love. Remember, I am with you always. Whatever you encounter, know that you will never face it alone in Jesus' name. It can be challenging to rise and start your day, but you are not alone. I will walk you through every step, one day at a time, my beloved. Take a deep breath and exhale slowly. There is no need to rush; everything unfolds in its own time. My Holy Spirit is with you, and I am for you. In the mighty name of Jesus, take authority over every enemy attack and cancel every demonic assignment.

Speak My Word over your life and your family. Rebuke any attacks on your marriage and any arguments brought by the enemy. Recognize these as lies and cast down every high thought that exalts itself against the knowledge of God. Bring every thought into captivity, making it obedient to Christ. Be ready to confront all disobedience with the obedience of Christ. Remember, what God has joined together, let no one separate.

JANUARY 26TH

The Enemy

> 2 Corinthians 10:5

We demolish arguments and every pretension that sets itself up against the knowledge of God, and we take captive every thought to make it obedient to Christ.

The Father is saying that the enemy is trying everything under the sun. He is attacking your relationships, marriages, and even your ministry. Pray and rebuke every demonic attack on your marriage, church, and your children and your children children. in the mighty name of Jesus. Cast down imaginations and every high thing that exalteth itself against God's knowledge and bring every thought into captivity to the obedience of Christ. Tell the devil you can't have my kids, you can't have my marriage, you have no power here. The victory is the Lord. I have victory because of Christ Jesus. Declare and decree that you have victory over every aspect in Jesus' name.

JANUARY 27ᵀᴴ

Healing and Forgiveness

Isaiah 53:3

He was despised and rejected by mankind,
a man of suffering and familiar with pain.
Like one from whom people hide their faces
he was despised, and we held him in low esteem.

2 Timothy 2:17

Their teaching will spread like gangrene. Among them are Hymenaeus and Philetus,

The Father is saying, "I was pierced for your transgressions, crushed for your iniquities; the punishment that brought you peace was upon Me, and by My stripes, you are healed." That illness or disease you face—be cured now in Jesus' name. Place your hand on the area that needs healing and command that sickness to be completely healed in the name of Jesus. It is by faith that you receive this complete healing.

If there is any unforgiveness in your heart, bring it before God now. Speak out loud that you forgive the person who has wronged you so nothing can block the healing or freedom I want to bring into your life. Unforgiveness is a barrier that hinders the healing and freedom I desire for you. Say, "Abba Father, I renounce any unforgiveness toward [person's name] and release them to You, Lord.

Unforgiveness can spread through your spirit like a disease. If you struggle to forgive, ask the Holy Spirit for grace, and I will freely give it to you, says the Lord your God.

JANUARY 28TH

Faith in Action

Romans 6:19

I am using an example from everyday life because of your human limitations. Just as you used to offer yourselves as slaves to impurity and to ever-increasing wickedness, so now offer yourselves as slaves to righteousness leading to holiness.

James 1:2-4

Consider it pure joy, my brothers and sisters,[a] whenever you face trials of many kinds, 3 because you know that the testing of your faith produces perseverance. 4 Let perseverance finish its work so that you may be mature and complete, not lacking anything.

The Father is saying, "You must take action by faith." Whatever you set out to do—writing a book, starting a business, pursuing law school, or simply holding onto a mustard seed of faith—must be done through faith. Every disciple in the Bible needed faith to accomplish their purpose; without faith, it is impossible to please God.

Though your flesh may resist My will, I remain forever faithful to fulfill My perfect plan for your life. I speak in human terms because of the weakness of your flesh. Just as you once offered parts of your body to impurity and lawlessness, now offer them as instruments of righteousness, leading to sanctification.

It is faith that pleases God. Remember that testing your faith produces perseverance. Allow perseverance to complete its work in you so that you may become mature and complete, not lacking anything. Trust in My faithfulness, and let your faith guide your actions.

JANUARY 29ᵀᴴ

Trust in the Lord Completely

Psalm 20:7

Some trust in chariots, and some in horses,

but we trust in the name of the Lord our God.

The Father is saying: "Trust in Me with all your heart, mind, and soul." When fear begins to creep in, it may be a sign that you've trusted Me with only certain aspects of your life. It's time to let go and let Me move in every area of your life.

You can place all your faith and trust in Me. Will you trust in Me alone? Ask My Holy Spirit to reveal those areas where you may not trust Me completely. As the Holy Spirit shows you these areas, say, "Jesus, I trust You with my children, my job, my career, and my finances. Relinquish it all to Me, place it in My hands, and leave it there. Watch as I turn it around for your good"

Some trust in chariots and horses, but we trust in the name of the Lord our God. Let this be your declaration as you surrender everything to Me.

JANUARY 30TH

Abide in Me

James 1:2

² Consider it pure joy, my brothers and sisters,[a] whenever you face trials of many kinds,

John 15:4

Remain in me, as I also remain in you. No branch can bear fruit by itself; it must remain in the vine. Neither can you bear fruit unless you remain in me.

Matthew 11:28-30

"Come to me, all you who are weary and burdened, and I will give you rest. ²⁹ Take my yoke upon you and learn from me, for I am gentle and humble in heart, and you will find rest for your souls. ³⁰ For my yoke is easy, and my burden is light."

The Father is saying, "Abide in Me, and I in you." Just as a branch cannot bear fruit by itself unless it remains connected to the vine, neither can you bear fruit unless you abide in Me. Continue to seek My face and My ways. Ask My Holy Spirit to teach you, for though you face hardships, I am always faithful.

I am omnipresent; I will never leave or forsake you, My beloved. Consider it pure joy, my brothers and sisters, whenever you face trials of many kinds. When the weight of life feels unbearable, begin to release those burdens to Me," says the Lord. "They were never yours to carry alone.

"Trust in Me wholeheartedly. 'Come to Me, all who are weary and burdened, and I will give you rest. Take My yoke upon you and learn from Me, for I am gentle and humble, and you will find rest for your souls. For My yoke is easy, and My burden is light.'"

FEBRUARY 1ˢᵀ

Put Your Hands On It

> Deuteronomy 30:9

Then the Lord your God will make you most prosperous in all the work of your hands and in the fruit of your womb, the young of your livestock, and the crops of your land. The Lord will again delight in you and make you prosperous, just as he delighted in your ancestors.

The Father is saying: "Put your hands on it." The Lord is calling you to take action in Jesus' name. If it's your business, put your hands on it. Your hands are anointed for such a time as this. If it's your job, put your hands on it. If it's your education, put your hands on it. I promise to bless it in Jesus' name.

All you need to do is put your hands on it and declare and decree that it is yours in Jesus' name. The enemy has been attacking you with fear and anxiety, but take authority over those spirits and cast them down to the abyss in Jesus' name. The devil is a liar! Rebuke every demonic attack on your mind and forget what the enemy is saying.

The enemy comes to steal, kill, and destroy, but I have come to give you life and life more abundantly. You are bearing much fruit in this season in Jesus' name; don't be concerned with your enemies. It doesn't matter what others say or what they intend to do. Where I'm taking you, your enemies can't follow. Pray for your enemies, but know your needs are already in your hands. It's time to use it in Jesus' name.

FEBRUARY 2ND

"Guard Your Heart and Lips"

❙ Proverbs 21:23

Those who guard their mouths and their tongues
keep themselves from calamity.

❙ Proverbs 4:23

Above all else, guard your heart,
for everything you do flows from it.

❙ Matthew 7:16

By their fruit, you will recognize them. Do people pick grapes from thornbushes, or figs from thistles?

❙ 1 Corinthians 15:33

Do not be misled: "Bad company corrupts good character."

The Father is saying, "Set a guard over your mouth; keep watch over the door of your lips. Keep yourself from gossiping. When others, even fellow believers, come to you with gossip, do not entertain it. Above all else, guard your heart; everything you do flows from it in Jesus' name." Be mindful of who you surround yourself with. "Do not be deceived. 'Bad company corrupts good character.' Not everyone is for you. Ask My Holy Spirit to increase your discernment so you'll know who has been sent by Me. By their fruit, you will recognize them. Do people pick grapes from thornbushes or figs from thistles?" Be vigilant. in guarding your heart and lips, for these are the gateways through which life and character flow.

FEBRUARY 3ʳᵈ

Hold On to God's Promises

2 Corinthians 1:20

For no matter how many promises God has made, they are "Yes" in Christ. And so through him the "Amen" is spoken by us to the glory of God.

Psalm 23:1-6

The Lord is my shepherd; I lack nothing.² He makes me lie down in green pastures, he leads me beside quiet waters, ³ he refreshes my soul. He guides me along the right paths for his name's sake.⁴ Even though I walk through the darkest valley,[a] I will fear no evil, for you are with me; your rod and your staff, they comfort me. You prepare a table before me in the presence of my enemies. You anoint my head with oil; my cup overflows. ⁶ Surely your goodness and love will follow me all the days of my life, and I will dwell in the house of the Lord forever.

The Father is saying, "Hold on to My promises for your life. My promises are yes and amen. These are promises from the living God, for no matter how many promises I have made, they are yes in Christ. And through Him, we speak the amen to the glory of God. Hallelujah!

You may face many trials but know I am always carrying you through the storm. Here is nothing I don't see or hear. My strength is within you. When you are weak, I am strong. Though you walk through the valley of the shadow of death, you will fear no evil, for I am with you. My rod and My staff comfort you. I prepare a table before you in the presence of your enemies; I anoint your head with oil and your cup overflows. Hold on to these promises, for they are your anchor in every season.

FEBRUARY 4ᵀᴴ

Evict Doubt and Embrace Faith

Proverbs 3:5

Trust in the Lord with all your heart and lean not on your own understanding;

Isaiah 55:8

"For my thoughts are not your thoughts,
neither are your ways my ways,"
declares the Lord.

What the Father is saying "Get rid of all doubt. Doubt can no longer occupy space in your heart. Today, serve the spirit of doubt an eviction notice. Renounce all doubt and unbelief, for they no longer have any place within you.

Ask My Holy Spirit to fill you from the crown of your head to the soles of your feet in Jesus' name.** Receive all that I have for you, My beloved. **Ask My Holy Spirit to increase your faith,** for your faith in Me alone will move mountains. Honestly, I tell you, if anyone says to this mountain, 'Go, throw yourself into the sea,' and does not doubt in their heart but believes that what they say will happen, it will be done for them." Your faith in Me increases as you trust Me wholeheartedly. **Do not depend on your understanding. My thoughts are not yours, nor are your ways My ways, declares the Lord.

Trust in Me with all of your heart, mind, and soul. Let faith replace doubt, and watch as I work wonders in your life.

FEBRUARY 5ᵀᴴ

Trust in My Presence and Promise

Genesis 28:15

I am with you and will watch over you wherever you go, and I will bring you back to this land. I will not leave you until I have done what I have promised you."

Psalm 28:7

The Lord is my strength and my shield;
my heart trusts in him, and he helps me.
My heart leaps for joy,
and with my song, I praise him.

The Father is saying, "I am with you and will watch over you wherever you go. I will bring you back to this land and not leave you until I have fulfilled My promise to you."

Do not listen to the lies of the enemy. Take every thought captive and make it obedient to Christ Jesus in His name. Not every thought is your own, so always ask the Holy Spirit to renew your mind as you spend time in the Word of God. Reading the Word of God will also renew your mind.

Come out of agreement with anything you've said about yourself or others that does not align with My truth. Life's issues and circumstances can easily weigh you down if you're not renewing your mind through the Word. **Release it all to Me and surrender your life and will.** Watch what I will do with your life.

Do not rely on your strength to navigate this journey. Pray, "Lord, I need You. Without You, I am nothing, but with You, I can do all things through Christ who gives me strength." The joy of the Lord is your strength. I am always with you, guiding you on the right path and using the right words at the right time.

FEBRUARY 6ᵀᴴ

Find Strength in Me

John 16:33

"I have told you these things so that in me you may have peace. In this world, you will have trouble. But take heart! I have overcome the world."

Hebrews 4:12

For the word of God is alive and active. Sharper than any double-edged sword, it penetrates even to dividing soul and spirit, joints and marrow; it judges the thoughts and attitudes of the heart.

The Father is saying, "I am your strength. You can do everything through Christ, who strengthens you in Jesus' name. There is no need to worry or fear, for I am with you, My beloved. No battle or storm is too big for Me, saith the Lord God. When you face a battle or storm, look at it and remind it of how big your God is. I am more powerful than any mountain you may face today."

Release every battle to Me. I have told you these things so you may have peace in Me. Yes, you will have trouble in this world, but take heart, My beloved; I have overcome the world.

Renew your mind daily in the Word of God. The Word of God is living and active, sharper than any double-edged sword; it penetrates even to dividing soul and spirit, joints and marrow; it judges the thoughts and attitudes of the heart. "Trust in My strength and find peace in My presence."

FEBRUARY 7ᵀᴴ

Give Me Your Brokenness

Matthew 10:22

You will be hated by everyone because of me, but the one who stands firm to the end will be saved.

The Father is saying, "Give Me all your brokenness and allow Me to fill you with My perfect peace." You will not find true peace, for I am the Prince of Peace. Though you may search for peace in people or habits, you will only see it in Me, saith the Lord.

Allow My presence to flow freely in you. "Freely you have received; freely give." Begin to release every burden and every broken part of you. I want all of you, not just part, but ALL." Ask My Holy Spirit to fill every broken part of you, and as you pray in the name of Jesus, "Ask My Holy Spirit to heal every aspect of your being."

When you minister to others, you won't be ministering out of a place of hurt or pain but from a place of healing and wholeness. Remember, "Everyone may hate you because of Me, but the one who stands firm will be saved in Jesus' name."

FEBRUARY 8TH

Break Free for Freedom

James 4:7

Submit yourselves, then, to God. Resist the devil, and he will flee from you.

The Father says to break free from that addiction. Break free from that mindset; break free from religion. Break free from the habits that keep you bound, for freedom is your portion. In Jesus' name. My desire for My children is for you all to be completely set free in Jesus' name.

Do not be deceived by the tactics of the enemy. The enemy wants you bound to that addiction, that bad habit, that lust, or even that idol you may not realize you have. But today, freedom is within your reach. Begin to repent and renounce everything that holds you back from the freedom I offer. Break free from all of it today in Jesus' name.

Repeat this prayer after Me:

Lord, I repent from idolizing anything or anyone other than You. I believe in You, Lord. I believe You died, were buried, and rose again on the third day. I turn to You and make You my Lord and Savior. I repent of all my sins, and I desire all of You. Come into my heart and life; invade every area in Jesus' name. I believe by faith that I can be delivered from all these things. I submit myself to You, God. I resist the devil; he will flee from me in Jesus' name. Amen.

Freedom is yours, beloved. Step into it today by faith.

FEBRUARY 9TH

Your Breakthrough is Coming

> James 2:26

As the body without the spirit is dead, so faith without deeds is dead.

> 2 Corinthians 10:5

We demolish arguments and every pretension that sets itself up against the knowledge of God, and we take captive every thought to make it obedient to Christ.

The Father is saying, Prepare for a breakthrough like never before. You've been asking for it, and now I am ready to break through that financial burden for you. In Jesus' name, I am tearing down every high thing that exalts itself against the knowledge of God. Get ready to receive all I have for you, my beloved—breakthroughs in your finances, marriage, and mind.

But understand this: a breakthrough isn't always about money or getting a new house. It's in your mental health, well-being, and Jesus' name. For some of you, the enemy has been attacking your mind, causing intense warfare in your thoughts. Call the Holy Spirit to send warring angels to fight on your behalf. Remember that I have angels encamped around you in My name when this happens.

I need you to have immense FAITH. Faith without works is dead. Repeat this prayer, my beloved:

I command every stronghold of fear and every curse to be broken off of my life in Jesus' name. I command every generational curse to be dismantled in the spirit realm in Jesus' name. By faith, I declare that these strongholds have been cast down in Jesus' name. I cast down imaginations and every high thing that exalts itself against the knowledge of God, bringing every thought into obedience to Christ Jesus. The enemy has no power over me or my life. Amen.

Your breakthrough is coming, beloved. Hold on to your faith, and watch how I move in your life.

FEBRUARY 10TH

Lay It All Down

Ephesians 6:12

For our struggle is not against flesh and blood but against the rulers, against the authorities, against the powers of this dark world, and against the spiritual forces of evil in the heavenly realms.

Galatians 5:22-23

But the fruit of the Spirit is love, joy, peace, forbearance, kindness, goodness, faithfulness, [23] gentleness, and self-control. Against such things, there is no law.

The Father is saying, Come and lay it all down at My feet—that stress, anxiety, and disappointment. Release it all to Me today. Don't carry it with you any longer. I see how you feel, believing that people are against you, but remember, our fight is not against flesh and blood. It's against principalities, powers, the rulers of darkness, and spiritual forces of evil in high places.

Understand that some people are influenced by spirits, and it's not truly them but the spirits operating behind them. When you feel attacked, pray for those people and ask My Holy Spirit to touch their hearts. The enemy wants you to hold on to bitterness and resentment. Still, I have called you to a higher way—to love and to bear the fruit of the Spirit: love, joy, peace, patience, kindness, goodness, faithfulness, and self-control.

Continue to pray for your enemies and seek My face. Trust that I will deal with them. Let go of the burden of holding onto hurt, and instead, walk in the freedom of My love.

FEBRUARY 11ᵀᴴ

Clear Your Mind and Heart

> Psalm 121:8

the Lord will watch over your coming and going

both now and forevermore.

> Psalm 32:8

I will instruct you and teach you in the way you should go;

I will counsel you with my loving eye on you.

The Father is saying, "Clear your mind from all the clutter that weighs you down. Ask My Holy Spirit to cleanse your mind and heart from all unrighteousness. I will watch over your coming and going, now and forever. That is My promise to you—hallelujah!"

The Holy Spirit will teach you My ways. I will instruct you and guide you in the path you should take. I will never leave you; you are never alone. Even when loneliness overwhelms you, remember that My Spirit dwells within you.

When the spirit of loneliness comes against you, take authority over it. Command every spirit of loneliness to be cast down to the abyss in the mighty name of Jesus. You are not alone, for I am with you always, guiding and protecting you.

FEBRUARY 12TH

Victory in the Midst of Struggle

Ephesians 3:16

I pray that out of his glorious riches, he may strengthen you with power through his Spirit in your inner being,

Hebrews 4:12

For the word of God is alive and active. Sharper than any double-edged sword, it penetrates even to dividing soul and spirit, joints and marrow; it judges the thoughts and attitudes of the heart.

The Father is saying, When you feel like you are losing, remember—you are winning. As My children, you are more than conquerors through Christ. The victory Jesus won is also yours in His mighty name.

My Spirit within you is strengthening your being. When you feel weak, ask My Holy Spirit to fortify every area of your life. My power will renew your mind, rejuvenate your body, and strengthen your inner being. I am a God of order, bringing everything into perfect alignment.

Consecrate yourself daily in My Word. The Word of God is alive and active, sharper than any two-edged sword, piercing the division of soul and spirit, joints and marrow, and discerning the thoughts and intentions of the heart.

When the enemy tries to corner you and attack you from every angle, **call out My name—JESUS! Command the devil to flee and be cast down to the abyss. **You hold the same power that raised Jesus from the dead,** and that power is inside you. You are victorious in Me.

FEBRUARY 13TH

Armor Up for the Day

Ephesians 6:11

Put on the full armor of God so you can take your stand against the devil's schemes.

The Father is saying, put on the whole armor of God so that you can stand firm against the devil's schemes. Wear the belt of truth, the breastplate of righteousness, and the gospel of peace to fit your feet with readiness. Take up the shield of faith to extinguish all the flaming arrows of the evil one, the helmet of salvation, and the sword of the Spirit, which is the Word of God. Pray in the Spirit on all occasions with all kinds of prayers and requests.

Each morning, before you leave your bed, make sure you put on the full armor of God. Wear it, live it, and breathe it. Without it, you cannot face the enemy in battle. Remember, no weapon formed against you shall prosper.

FEBRUARY 14TH

Fully Surrendered to the Lord

John 4:14

but whoever drinks the water I give them will never thirst. Indeed, the water I give them will become in them a spring of water welling up to eternal life."

Isaiah 45:3

I will give you hidden treasures,
riches stored in secret places,
so that you may know that I am the Lord,
the God of Israel, who summons you by name

Psalm 24:9

Lift up your heads, you gates;
lift them up, you ancient doors,
that the King of glory may come in.

What the Father is saying is, give yourself entirely to me. Trust in the Lord, and I will help you; you will no longer thirst or go hungry. I will satisfy you. The water I give will become a spring of water welling up to eternal life.

When you begin to feel spiritually dull, ask yourself from which well you are drinking. Are you drinking from the living water of Christ or the world and its pleasures? I will give you hidden treasures and riches stored in secret places so that you may know I am the God of Israel, who summons you by name. Praise my holy name, for I am holy. Lift your heads, you gates; lift them, you ancient doors, that the King of Glory may come in.

FEBRUARY 15ᵀᴴ

Embrace Childlike Faith

James 1:6-8

But when you ask, you must believe and not doubt because the one who doubts is like a wave of the sea, blown and tossed by the wind. ⁷ That person should not expect to receive anything from the Lord. ⁸ Such a person is double-minded and unstable in all they do.

Matthew 18:2-4

He called a little child to him and placed the child among them.³ And he said: "Truly I tell you, unless you change and become like little children, you will never enter the kingdom of heaven.⁴ Therefore, whoever takes the lowly position of this child is the greatest in the kingdom of heaven.

Philippians 4:6

He called a little child to him and placed the child among them.³ And he said: "Truly I tell you, unless you change and become like little children, you will never enter the kingdom of heaven.⁴ Therefore, whoever takes the lowly position of this child is the greatest in the kingdom of heaven.

What the Father is saying is true: unless you change and become like little children, you will never enter the kingdom of heaven. Come to me with childlike faith. Ask my Holy Spirit to remove any blockages or barriers holding you back. Doubt can hinder your faith, so do not be undecided and unstable like a wave tossed by the wind. You must have faith and trust in what I am telling you, my beloved.

Continue to seek me with your heart, mind, and soul. Life and responsibilities sometimes feel overwhelming, but instead of flustering, let me help carry those burdens. You are not meant to carry them alone. Ask my Holy Spirit to assist you in managing these tasks. I will give you peace that surpasses all understanding, which will guard your hearts and minds in Christ Jesus.

FEBRUARY 16TH

Renew Your Mind

John 10:27-28

My sheep listen to my voice; I know them, and they follow me.²⁸ I give them eternal life, and they shall never perish; no one will snatch them out of my hand.

The Father is saying to renew your mind in the Word of God. Focus on Him, not on the distractions around you. Don't look to the left or the right. Don't worry about what's going wrong or what isn't working out. Something that didn't work out may be a blessing in disguise.

Focus on me and meditate on every word I've spoken over your life. The enemy likes to bring confusion, making you think I didn't speak that over your life. He may even convince you it's not my voice you're hearing. But that is a lie straight from the pit. I'm confirming with you now: it is my voice you hear, whether it's a thought, a word from God, or even an audible voice. I speak to all of my children in different ways. Come deeper with me. My sheep hear my voice; I know them, and they follow me.

FEBRUARY 17TH

Waiting on God

James 1:4

Let perseverance finish its work so that you may be mature and complete, not lacking anything.

The Father is saying, "Wait before me as you worship." You may feel as though you are wandering in the wilderness, but I see you. You are not alone. You are on the brink of rising higher. You followed my call when you left your home and your past behind. Although you might feel stuck, remember you are not. My grace is sufficient for you. I am strengthening you as you have asked. Trust that everything unfolding in your life is according to my plan. Though your flesh may grow weak, my Spirit remains strong within you. My presence dwells in you, empowering you to persevere. Let perseverance complete its work in you so that you may be mature, complete, and lacking nothing.

FEBRUARY 18TH

Standing Firm in Your Calling

James 4:7

Submit yourselves, then, to God. Resist the devil, and he will flee from you.

Isaiah 41:9-10

I took you from the ends of the earth; from its farthest corners, I called you. I said, 'You are my servant'; I have chosen you and have not rejected you. So do not fear, for I am with you; do not be dismayed, for I am your God. I will strengthen you and help you; I will uphold you with my righteous right hand.

The Father is saying, "Do not let your circumstances define you or who I have called you to be." Be persistent and guard against the lies of the enemy. Cast down every spirit of deception in the name of Jesus. Submit yourselves to me, resist the devil, and he will flee you. I have chosen you for this time. You are my beloved, and I have not rejected you. Do not fear, for I am with you. Do not be dismayed, for I am your God. I will strengthen, help, and uphold you with my righteous right hand. Ask my Holy Spirit to renew your strength and shift your perspective. Seek to see others and situations through my eyes, my beloved.

FEBRUARY 19TH

Drawing Near to the Unknown God

Acts 17:23-24

For as I walked around and looked carefully at your objects of worship, I even found an altar with this inscription: to an unknown god. So you are ignorant of the very thing you worship—and this is what I am going to proclaim to you. 24"The God who made the world and everything in it is the Lord of heaven and earth and does not live in temples built by human hands.

The Father is saying, "Come to me with an open heart." I am here, ready to listen to you, my beloved. I will never leave you. Even if you feel I am distant, know I am closer than you realize. As I have observed your worship, I noticed an altar inscribed 'to an unknown God.' You may not fully understand whom you worship. I want to reveal this: The God who created the world and everything in it is the Lord of heaven and earth and does not dwell in temples made by human hands. Honor Christ as holy in your heart. Let this be reflected in your behavior, words, and thoughts, for Jesus is Lord.

FEBRUARY 20ᵀᴴ

The Gift of Lasting Peace

> Philippians 4:7

And the peace of God, which transcends all understanding, will guard your hearts and your minds in Christ Jesus.

> Jeremiah 33:6

Nevertheless, I will bring health and healing to it; I will heal my people and will let them enjoy abundant peace and security.

The Father is saying, "When you begin to experience my peace, you should recognize it as a blessing from me." True peace comes from above. 'And the peace of God, which surpasses all understanding, will guard your hearts and minds in Christ Jesus.' The world's riches are fleeting and will not endure, but the peace I give you lasts forever. This peace is true wealth, a blessing from God. I will bring you health and healing, revealing an abundance of peace and truth, my beloved."

FEBRUARY 21ST

Embracing God's Strength in Every Challenge

> Joshua 3:5

Joshua told the people, "Consecrate yourselves, for tomorrow the Lord will do amazing things among you."

> Proverbs 18:10

The name of the Lord is a fortified tower; the righteous run to it and are safe.

The Father is saying, "Release the illusion of a problem-free life. Obstacles, hardships, and pressures are part of your journey, but you do not face them alone." The Holy Spirit dwells within you as your helper and advocate. The Holy Spirit will guide you through no matter the mountains or difficulties you encounter. You will not remain stuck in Jesus' name. Dedicate yourself to the word of God, as Joshua instructed the people: 'Consecrate yourselves, for tomorrow the Lord will do wonders among you.' Align all you do with the Lord. He is your strength and refuge; His name is a strong tower where the righteous find safety.

FEBRUARY 22ND

Numbers 23:19

God is not human, that he should lie, not a human being, that he should change his mind. Does he speak and then not act? Does he promise and not fulfill?

The Father is saying, "Release every disappointment and betrayal to me." Do not let your emotions lead you. At the same time, your feelings may fluctuate, but remember that I remain unchanged. My promises to you are unwavering and true. Every word I have spoken over your life is yes and amen. Do not be deceived by the enemy's tactics of distraction and confusion, which are lies from the pit of hell. I will guide you through this; I am the Waymaker. What truly matters is my unchanging nature and my promises. I am not a man who should lie or change my mind. If I have spoken, I will surely bring it to pass.

FEBRUARY 23ᴿᴰ

Approaching the Throne with Boldness

Hebrews 4:16

Let us then approach God's throne of grace with confidence so that we may receive mercy and find grace to help us in our time of need.

1 Timothy 6:15

which God will bring about in his own time—God, the blessed and only Ruler, the King of kings and Lord of Lords,

Psalm 27:1

The Lord is my light and my salvation— whom shall I fear? The Lord is the stronghold of my life— of whom shall I be afraid?

The Father is saying, "Come boldly to me. Let us confidently approach God's throne of grace so we may receive mercy and find grace in our time of need." Seek the Holy Spirit for boldness—to preach the gospel and to fulfill my will in Jesus' name. Come to me assured of your identity in me. I am the King of Kings, the Lord of Lords, the Alpha and Omega, the beginning and the end. Even if you feel unqualified for the task, remember that I qualify, not man. I have called you by name and appointed you for this moment. Do not be afraid. The Lord is your light and salvation; whom shall you fear? The Lord is the stronghold of your life; of whom shall you be afraid?

FEBRUARY 24ᵀᴴ

Anticipating God's Abundant Blessings

Joel 2:25

"I will repay you for the years the locusts have eaten— the great locust and the young locust, the other locusts and the locust swarm— my great army that I sent among you.

Deuteronomy 28:7

The Lord will grant that the enemies who rise up against you will be defeated before you. They will come at you from one direction but flee from you in seven.

The Father is saying, "What I am about to do for you is beyond what ears have heard or eyes have seen." I am preparing to open the floodgates of heaven on your behalf. You have humbled yourself before the Almighty God, and while others may have overlooked you, I have included you in my plans. When your enemies rose against you, I scattered them. There is nothing I am unwilling to do for you. Even when you felt like giving up, I provided the grace you needed to fulfill my will. My presence accompanies you wherever you go. I will restore what has been lost, repaying you for the years the locusts have consumed—every type of locust and the great army I sent against you.

FEBRUARY 25ᵀᴴ

Strength in Weakness

2 Corinthians 12: 8-10

⁸ Three times I pleaded with the Lord to take it away from me. ⁹ But he said to me, "My grace is sufficient for you, for my power is made perfect in weakness." Therefore, I will boast all the more gladly about my weaknesses so that Christ's power may rest on me. ¹⁰ That is why, for Christ's sake, I delight in weaknesses, in insults, in hardships, in persecutions, in difficulties. For when I am weak, then I am strong.

The Father is saying, "When you are under attack, remember that you are a threat to the enemy." The adversary, the devil, has already been defeated, and victory is yours, my beloved. Rejoice and be glad, for you are walking in my perfect will. I will never let you down. I understand that the enemy often attacks when you are weak, but remember my words: 'My grace is sufficient for you, for my strength is made perfect in weakness.' Embrace your weaknesses, reproaches, needs, persecutions, and distress for Christ's sake. When you are weak, you are strong. Please do not rely on your own strength; it will fail, but my strength is made perfect in your weakness.

FEBRUARY 26TH

Staying Alert Against the Enemy

1 Peter 5:8

Be alert and of sober mind. Your enemy, the devil, prowls around like a roaring lion, looking for someone to devour.

The Father says, "Be vigilant and have a clear mind, for your enemy, the devil, prowls around like a roaring lion, seeking someone to devour." When confusion and discord arise, speak the word of God aloud to stand firm against the enemy's attacks. The word of God is truth and your defense. Even if you feel I am far away, know I am with you and will never leave your side. The Holy Spirit will guide and lead you on the right path. When in doubt, seek the Holy Spirit's guidance, and He will reassure you of the direction.

FEBRUARY 27th

Guarding Your Mind Against Deception

2 Corinthians 10:5

We demolish arguments and every pretension that sets itself up against the knowledge of God, and we take captive every thought to make it obedient to Christ.

Psalm 110:1

The Lord says to my Lord: "Sit at my right hand until I make your enemies a footstool for your feet."

The Father is saying, "Not every thought that crosses your mind is your own." Ask the Holy Spirit to take every thought captive and obey Christ Jesus. Seek His help to cleanse your mind from unrighteous thinking. You are called to cast down imaginations and every high thing that exalts itself against the knowledge of God, bringing every thought into captivity to the obedience of Christ. The enemy tries to lead you into agreement with lies from the pit of hell. Break free by declaring, 'I come out of every contract and lie of the enemy in Jesus' name.' Reject every word curse in the spirit and command every lie to be demolished in Jesus' name. Remember, the Lord says, 'Sit at my right hand until I make your enemies a footstool for your feet.

FEBRUARY 28TH

Exchanging Burdens for Peace

1 Peter 5:7

Cast all your anxiety on him because he cares for you.

Philippians 4:7

And the peace of God, which transcends all understanding, will guard your hearts and your minds in Christ Jesus.

The Father is saying, "Cast all your anxiety on me because I care deeply for you, my beloved." Surrender everything—your past, present, and future—to me. Allow me to carry your burdens, for there is nothing you face that I do not already know about. Release each burden to me, one by one, as they were never meant for you to bear alone. I will provide you with peace amidst it all. Exchange your cares, concerns, and anxieties for my perfect peace that surpasses all understanding. Even amid complexity, you will experience a peace that makes no sense to the world. Trust in me alone; my peace will guard your hearts and minds in Christ Jesus. Approach me with thanksgiving, and thank me for what I have done and am about to do in Jesus' name.

FEBRUARY 29ᵀᴴ

Obedience in Separation

Exodus 34:14

Do not worship any other god, for the Lord, whose name is Jealous, is a jealous God.

Luke 17:32

Remember Lot's wife!

The Father is saying, "You have heard me correctly, my beloved. I have asked you to separate yourself from certain family members and specific areas, providing clear directions on your path." I understand this is challenging, but you can do everything through Christ Jesus, who strengthens you. Even when you feel alone, remember you are never truly alone. Your obedience will have a lasting impact, saving generations. This is why you cannot bring them with you. Follow my commands diligently, for I am your Lord. It is crucial to heed the call placed upon your life. I have set you apart to reveal visions and dreams to you. 'You shall worship no other god, for the Lord, whose name is Jealous, is a jealous God.' Step away from those hindering your mission and focus on doing my will. Do not look back or be like Lot's wife, who turned into a pillar of salt by looking behind.

MARCH 1ST

Relinquishing Fear and Embracing Freedom

Isaiah 59:1

Surely the arm of the Lord is not too short to save, nor his ear too dull to hear.

Matthew 3:2-12

"Repent, for the kingdom of heaven has come near."³ This is he who was spoken of through the prophet Isaiah: "A voice of one calling in the wilderness, 'Prepare the way for the Lord, make straight paths for him.'" ⁴ John's clothes were made of camel's hair, and he had a leather belt around his waist. His food was locusts and wild honey.⁵ People went out to him from Jerusalem and all Judea and the whole region of the Jordan. ⁶ Confessing their sins, they were baptized by him in the Jordan River.⁷ But when he saw many of the Pharisees and Sadducees coming to where he was baptizing, he said to them: "You brood of vipers! Who warned you to flee from the coming wrath? ⁸ Produce fruit in keeping with repentance. ⁹ And do not think you can say to yourselves, 'We have Abraham as our father.' I tell you that out of these stones God can raise up children for Abraham. ¹⁰ The ax is already at the root of the trees, and every tree that does not produce good fruit will be cut down and thrown into the fire.¹¹ "I baptize you with[b] water for repentance. But after me comes one who is more powerful than I, whose sandals I am not worthy to carry. He will baptize you with[c] the Holy Spirit and fire. ¹² His winnowing fork is in his hand, and he will clear his threshing floor, gathering his wheat into the barn and burning up the chaff with unquenchable fire."

The Father is saying, "Relinquish all fear and doubt and come to me with expectancy. I will deliver you from the hand of the enemy." The arm of the Lord is not too short to save, nor is His ear too dull to hear. Repent all your sins, and today, you will receive freedom from every form of bondage. Change your mind and turn away from the old ways, for the kingdom of heaven is near. This is the fulfillment of what was spoken by the prophet Isaiah: 'The voice of one crying in the wilderness: Prepare the way of the Lord, make His paths straight.

MARCH 2ND

Moving Forward with Forgiveness

Romans 8:1

Therefore, there is now no condemnation for those who are in Christ Jesus,

Philippians 3:12-14

Not that I have already obtained all this or have already arrived at my goal, but I press on to take hold of that for which Christ Jesus took hold of me. ¹³ Brothers and sisters, I do not consider myself yet to have taken hold of it. But one thing I do: Forgetting what is behind and straining toward what is ahead, ¹⁴ I press on toward the goal to win the prize for which God has called me heavenward in Christ Jesus.

The Father is saying, "I have already forgiven you, so there is no need for self-condemnation." There is no condemnation for those who are in Christ Jesus. You have repented your sin, and it is time to move forward. Condemnation comes from the adversary, not from me. I am for you, not against you, constantly fighting for you. Although you may not have achieved perfection, continue pressing on, just as I press on to claim what Christ Jesus has made me His own. Forget what lies behind and focus on what lies ahead. Press on toward the goal for the prize of the upward call of God in Christ Jesus.

MARCH 3ʳᴰ

Embracing Limitless Faith

> Matthew 17:20

He replied, "Because you have so little faith. Truly, I tell you, if you have faith as small as a mustard seed, you can say to this mountain, 'Move from here to there,' and it will move. Nothing will be impossible for you."

The Father is saying, "Do not doubt what I can accomplish in your life." Do you have faith that I can do it? I am the God of Abraham, Isaac, and Jacob. Remove the limits you have placed on me, for I am a limitless God. I ask that you place your faith in me and remain obedient, for obedience is greater than sacrifice. Faith as small as a mustard seed can move mountains, and nothing will be impossible for you. Faith pleases me; without it, it is impossible to please me. Ask the Holy Spirit to increase your faith and remove anything not of me, in Jesus' name.

MARCH 4TH

Responding with Grace

> Proverbs 25:21-23

If your enemy is hungry, give him food to eat; if he is thirsty, give him water to drink. ²² In doing this, you will heap burning coals on his head, and the Lord will reward you. ²³ Like a north wind that brings unexpected rain is a sly tongue—which provokes a horrified look.

The Father is saying, "If your enemy is hungry, provide him with food; if he is thirsty, give him water to drink." By doing this, you will heap burning coals on his head, and I, the Lord, will reward you. It is not important what your enemies have done or are doing. Remember, I am an all-knowing God who sees and understands everything. I am with you. When your enemies are in need, show them kindness, and I will reward your faithfulness.

MARCH 5TH

Setting Your Mind on Heavenly Thing

Colossians 3:2

Set your minds on things above, not on earthly things.

The Father is saying, "Set your mind on things above, not on earthly matters." For you have died, and your life is now hidden with Christ in God. When Christ appears in your life, you will also appear with Him in glory. By focusing on heavenly things, everything else will fade away, your faith will grow, and the enemy's attacks will be dismantled in the spirit. This focus allows you to experience the true joy and blessings I desire to lavish upon and through you."

MARCH 6ᵀᴴ

Seeking God with a Whole Heart

Matthew 7:7

"Ask and it will be given to you; seek and you will find; knock and the door will be opened to you.

Galatians 5:22-23

²² But the fruit of the Spirit is love, joy, peace, forbearance, kindness, goodness, faithfulness, ²³ gentleness and self-control. Against such things, there is no law.

The Father is saying, "When you come to me, seek me with your whole heart, mind, and soul." Ask, and it will be given to you; seek, and you will find me; knock, and the door will be opened to you. Anything you ask in my name will be granted. Request the Holy Spirit to remove all unbelief and to increase your faith in every area of your life. The fruits of the Spirit—love, joy, peace, patience, kindness, goodness, gentleness, faithfulness, and self-control—will grow abundantly in my name. Remember, you can do nothing apart from me, my beloved."

MARCH 7ᵀᴴ

A Promise of Renewal

> Romans 8:28

²⁸ And we know that in all things God works for the good of those who love him, who have been called according to his purpose.

The Father is saying that you should approach Him with anticipation and faith, trusting that He has great things in store for you. It's natural to feel disheartened when you don't see immediate changes or progress, but know that a breakthrough is near.

This breakthrough will touch every area of your life—mental health, finances, relationships, and more. Though the journey may have felt rough and challenging, it is all part of His divine plan. God is shaping you, removing what isn't beneficial, and orchestrating everything for your good.

As you seek His guidance, remember to consult the Holy Spirit for direction. Don't be swayed by your own feelings or perceptions, but rely on the Holy Spirit to reveal what is best for you. Trust in His wisdom to guide your steps and lead you through this transformative season.

MARCH 8ᵀᴴ

Remembering His Sacrifice

1 Corinthians 11: 23-26

²³ For I received from the Lord what I also passed on to you: The Lord Jesus, on the night he was betrayed, took bread, ²⁴ and when he had given thanks, he broke it and said, "This is my body, which is for you; do this in remembrance of me." ²⁵ In the same way, after supper, he took the cup, saying, "This cup is the new covenant in my blood; do this, whenever you drink it, in remembrance of me." ²⁶ For whenever you eat this bread and drink this cup, you proclaim the Lord's death until he comes.

The Father is saying that Jesus invites us to partake in communion as a powerful act of remembrance. The bread and the cup are not merely symbols but are deeply significant reminders of His sacrifice for humanity. The bread represents His body, broken for us, while the cup signifies His blood, shed for the new covenant.

As Paul recounts, on the night Jesus was betrayed, He took bread, gave thanks, broke it, and said, "This is my body, which is for you; do this in remembrance of me." In the same way, He took the cup after supper, declaring, "This cup is the new covenant in my blood; do this, as often as you drink it, in remembrance of me."

Communion is a time to honor His sacrifice and proclaim His death until He returns. Each time we eat the bread and drink the cup, we reaffirm our faith and remember the profound cost of His love.

MARCH 9TH

A Call to Surrender

Luke 11:25

When it arrives, it finds the house swept clean and put in order.

Proverbs 24:3-4

By wisdom, a house is built, and through understanding, it is established; ⁴ through knowledge, its rooms are filled with rare and beautiful treasures.

Psalm 51:10

Create in me a pure heart, O God, and renew a steadfast spirit within me.

The Father is saying, "It's time." It's time to surrender every part of your life to Him—your will, ways, and heart. Trust in Him with your whole being and remove all distractions that hinder your walk with Him.

For some, this means letting go of certain people. For others, it involves breaking free from worldly addictions or overcoming detrimental habits. If you've been seeking confirmation, here it is: the Lord calls you to end old cycles and embrace His order and peace.

It is time for breakthrough after breakthrough and an overflow of His presence in your life. Embrace this moment of transformation and renewal, knowing that God is preparing you for greater things.

MARCH 10TH

Unbounded Provision

> Ephesians 3:20

Now to him who is able to do immeasurably more than all we ask or imagine, according to his power that is at work within us,

The Father is saying that He promises to meet every need you have—physical, emotional, spiritual, or mental—without limit. He invites you to remove any constraints you've placed on His ability to provide and to trust Him for abundant blessings in Jesus' name. Ask the Holy Spirit to fill you if you need strength or grace for today. Embrace the reality of having a loving Father in heaven who adores you and can exceed your wildest dreams and expectations. Let go of any feeling of being fatherless and trust in His boundless provision and care.

MARCH 11ᵀᴴ

Triumph in the Midst of Trials

> Revelation 5:5

Then one of the elders said to me, "Do not weep! See, the Lion of the tribe of Judah, the Root of David, has triumphed. He is able to open the scroll and its seven seals."

The Father is saying that just as the elder in Revelation proclaimed, "Do not weep; the Lion of the tribe of Judah, the Root of David, has triumphed." He alone is worthy to open the scroll and its seven seals. Do not fret or fear, for the Lord your God is with you and for you. He accompanies you wherever you go. Continue to seek Him and invite His presence into every area of your life. Though you may face various trials, remember that these are not strange occurrences but opportunities to share in Christ's sufferings. Rejoice, for as you participate in His trials, you will also share His glory with exceeding joy. Ask the Holy Spirit to reveal more profound truths and take you further into the things of God. You and the Lord will explore the depths of His presence and promises.

MARCH 12ᵀᴴ

Breaking Down Strongholds

> 2 Corinthians 10:4

The weapons we fight with are not the weapons of the world. On the contrary, they have divine power to demolish strongholds.

> 1 Corinthians 2:16

For, "Who has known the mind of the Lord so as to instruct him?" But we have the mind of Christ.

The Father is saying, "Our weapons of warfare are not earthly but powerful through God for demolishing strongholds." These strongholds can take root in your mind or any area of your life where you repeatedly entertain and agree with negative or deceptive thoughts, granting the enemy access. To close this door, renounce and rebuke every lie you've accepted. If you struggle with beliefs such as always being poor or never reaching your full potential, recognize these as lies from the enemy. Renounce them and ask the Holy Spirit to dismantle these strongholds in your mind. Remember, we have the mind of Christ and should not let the enemy use our thoughts or lives for his purposes. Instead, declare and decree God's Word over your mind and life, affirming your identity as a child of God.

MARCH 13TH

Finding Peace in the Secret Place

Matthew 6:6

But when you pray, go into your room, close the door, and pray to your Father, who is unseen. Then your Father, who sees what is done in secret, will reward you.

John 14:27

Peace I leave with you; my peace I give you. I do not give to you as the world gives. Do not let your hearts be troubled, and do not be afraid.

The Father is saying, "Find solace in your secret place of prayer." Go into your room, close the door, and speak to your unseen Father. He sees what is done in secret and will reward you. In this quiet space, immerse yourself in His presence. The Father delights in spending time with you and cherishes your presence. He longs to be close to you and offers you His peace, which surpasses all understanding and is not found in the world. Whatever burdens you carry, lay them down at His feet. He gives you peace of mind and heart, a gift that dispels fear and trouble. Embrace His peace and draw near to Him in this sacred time.

MARCH 14TH

Guarded by His Angels

Psalm 91:11

For he will command his angels concerning you to guard you in all your ways;

The Father is saying that He has given His angels charge over you to protect you in all your ways. Wherever you go, angels are assigned to guard and support you. They will catch you if you stumble, ensuring you do not fall. You will walk safely even among dangers, such as lions and snakes, with divine protection guiding your path. The angels have been commanded to act on your behalf and will assist you whenever needed. Trust in their presence and authority, knowing you are surrounded by heavenly guardians.

MARCH 15TH

With You Always

Acts 12:17

Peter motioned with his hand for them to be quiet and described how the Lord had brought him out of prison. "Tell James and the other brothers and sisters about this," he said, and then he left for another place.

Isaiah 43:4

Since you are precious and honored in my sight, and because I love you,

I will give people in exchange for you, nations in exchange for your life.

The Father is saying that He is with you when you rise and lie down. He continually calls you to a deeper relationship with Him, inviting you to ascend to new heights. You are precious and beloved in His sight. Ask the Holy Spirit to reveal how God sees you—beautiful and perfect, just as you are. Just as the Lord brought Peter out of prison and instructed him to share the news, so too is He guiding and urging you to embrace the depth of His love and presence. Trust that He is always with you, leading you forward in His grace.

MARCH 16th

Trusting Fully

2 Corinthians 12:7

or because of these surpassingly great revelations. Therefore, in order to keep me from becoming conceited, I was given a thorn in my flesh, a messenger of Satan, to torment me.

Proverbs 3:5-6

Trust in the Lord with all your heart and lean not on your own understanding; 6 in all your ways submit to him, and he will make your paths straight.

The Father is saying, "Will you trust Me with all your heart?" Will you surrender that addiction that binds you or release the family member who holds you back? Remember, He cares for them too. He desires all of you—not just part, but your whole self. Trust in His guidance, knowing He will lead you on the right path. Your weaknesses are an opportunity for His strength to shine through. Ask the Holy Spirit to strengthen and renew your soul in Jesus' name, embracing the fullness of His support and grace.

MARCH 17TH

Exalting the Name Above All Names

> Matthew 6: 25-34

"Therefore, I tell you, do not worry about your life, what you will eat or drink, or about your body, what you will wear. Is not life more than food and the body more than clothes? **26** Look at the birds of the air; they do not sow or reap or store away in barns, and yet your heavenly Father feeds them. Are you not much more valuable than they? **27** Can any one of you, by worrying, add a single hour to your life? **28** "And why do you worry about clothes? See how the flowers of the field grow. They do not labor or spin. **29** Yet I tell you that not even Solomon in all his splendor was dressed like one of these.**30** If that is how God clothes the grass of the field, which is here today and tomorrow is thrown into the fire, will he not much more clothe you—you of little faith? **31** So do not worry, saying, 'What shall we eat?' or 'What shall we drink?' or 'What shall we wear?'**32** For the pagans run after all these things, and your heavenly Father knows that you need them. **33** But seek first his kingdom and his righteousness, and all these things will be given to you as well. **34** Therefore do not worry about tomorrow, for tomorrow will worry about itself. Each day has enough trouble of its own.

The Father is saying that you should bow before Him and exalt His name, which is above every other name. Jesus is the Alpha and the Omega, the beginning and the end, the King of Kings and the Lord of Lords. He is the God of the impossible and calls you to remove all limits you've placed on Him. He is a boundless God who will provide for all your needs. There is no need to worry about tomorrow, as it will take care of itself. Focus on today, and release your concerns about finances, family, and other burdens into His hands. Trust that it is better in His hands than in yours, for each day has enough troubles of its own.

MARCH 18TH

Come As You Are

1 John 1:4

We write this to make our joy complete.

The Father is saying that you should come to Him just as you are—broken, depressed, or struggling with any problem or addiction. He doesn't require you to be fixed or cleaned before coming to Him. His love is unconditional, and He welcomes you with open arms. Your surrender to Him, in whatever state you find yourself, is more than enough. He does not count your sins against you; once you repent and turn to Him, He forgives and wipes your sins away completely. As Scripture says, if we confess our sins, He will forgive us and cleanse us from all unrighteousness. The Father is here to restore and heal you. Come to Him without hesitation or pretense.

MARCH 19ᵀᴴ

You Are Mine

Isaiah 43:1-2

But now, this is what the Lord says— he who created you, Jacob, he who formed you, Israel: "Do not fear, for I have redeemed you; I have summoned you by name; you are mine. ² When you pass through the waters, I will be with you; and when you pass through the rivers, they will not sweep over you. When you walk through the fire, you will not be burned; the flames will not set you ablaze.

The Father is saying that you should not fear, for He has redeemed and called you by name. You belong to Him, and He belongs to you. Whether you pass through waters or rivers, He will be with you, and they will not overwhelm you. His presence is constant, regardless of your emotions— whether you are down or joyful, His love remains steadfast. God is love itself, and His commitment to you is unchanging. He will never leave or forsake you; you are held securely in the palm of His hand. You are dearly loved and never alone.

MARCH 20ᵀᴴ

Stand Firm in Faith

Romans 12:12

Be joyful in hope, patient in affliction, faithful in prayer.

1 Peter 1:3

Praise be to the God and Father of our Lord Jesus Christ! In his great mercy he has given us new birth into a living hope through the resurrection of Jesus Christ from the dead,

The Father is saying that you should not give up, even though the enemy works hard to corner you. The adversary may use your coworkers, family members, or even people who seem friendly but are influenced without their awareness. Stay alert, and do not let the devil manipulate or frighten you. Remember, through Jesus Christ, you have all power and authority. Rebuke every attack from the enemy immediately and bind it in Jesus' name. Do not wait—act swiftly when challenges arise. You are a warrior anointed for this time. Keep your focus on the Father, placing all your hope in Him. You will never lose hope by entrusting it to Him, for He is the way, the truth, and the life. Embrace the power in the name of Jesus.

MARCH 21ST

Remain Steadfast

Joel 2:25

"I will repay you for the years the locusts have eaten— the great locust and the young locust, the other locusts and the locust swarm— my great army that I sent among you.

The Father is saying you should not give up or be swayed by the enemy's lies. Rebuke every spirit of deception and resist believing the falsehoods the devil tries to plant in your mind and life. Remember that the Holy Spirit dwells within you, sent to comfort and guide you at any moment of need. Ask the Holy Spirit for guidance if you ever feel distant from God. You may be led to fast or take other steps as directed. Continue to seek God's presence and ways, learning to depend on Him fully. He has asked you to let go of certain things not because He is withholding but because they cannot accompany you to the next level of His plan for your life. Be obedient and trust in His guidance as He leads you forward.

MARCH 22ND

You Are Not Alone

John 20:21

Again, Jesus said, "Peace be with you! As the Father has sent me, I am sending you."

Psalm 23:2

He makes me lie down in green pastures, he leads me beside quiet waters,

The Father is saying, "You are not alone. Surrender everything to Him, for He is ready to restore and bring you back into order." Even if you don't feel it, trust that He is working according to His promises and aligning you with His will. Do not hold back; offer all of yourself to Him. He will restore what has been taken from you, returning it a hundredfold in the name of Jesus. The Father will repay you for the years of loss and hardship, whether from locusts or any other trial. Trust in His power to renew and bless you abundantly.

MARCH 23ᴿᴰ

Peace Be With You

John 20:21

Again, Jesus said, "Peace be with you! As the Father has sent me, I am sending you."

Psalm 23:2

He makes me lie down in green pastures, he leads me beside quiet waters,

The Father is saying that you that you are in perfect peace. Just as Jesus declared, "Peace be with you," He speaks shalom over you—bringing peace to your mind, heart, and family. He is continually at work in your life, even behind the scenes, orchestrating everything for your good out of His deep love for you. Trust that He sees your wholehearted trust and will guide you beside still waters, restoring your soul and leading you in righteousness for His name's sake.

MARCH 24™

Surrender and Transformation

> Galatians 2:20

I have been crucified with Christ, and I no longer live, but Christ lives in me. The life I now live in the body, I live by faith in the Son of God, who loved me and gave himself for me.

The Father is saying that you need to surrender your life to Him. When you do, you declare you no longer own your life. You have asked Him to remove worldly influences. He is faithfully burning away selfish desires and wickedness, setting you apart. Though you remain in this world, you are no longer defined by it. Your life is now lived by faith in the Son of God, who loved you and gave Himself for you. Embrace this new identity and commit to moving forward in this transformed state, not returning to your old ways.

MARCH 25ᵀᴴ

God's Unfailing Presence

> Deuteronomy 31:8

The Lord himself goes before you and will be with you; he will never leave you nor forsake you. Do not be afraid; do not be discouraged."

The Father is saying, "The Lord Himself goes before you and will be with you always. He will never leave you nor forsake you." Even when things don't go as planned and circumstances seem challenging, let go of the need to control every situation and the expectation of a problem-free life. Trust that God has all the power and works everything out for your good. As His beloved, He will never let you down. Instead of being discouraged by unmet expectations, believe He has something far better in store for you than you could ask or imagine. Seek guidance and clarity from the Holy Spirit on the direction to take in every area of your life.

MARCH 26TH

Restoration After Suffering

> 1 Peter 5:10-11

And the God of all grace, who called you to his eternal glory in Christ, after you have suffered a little while, will himself restore you and make you strong, firm, and steadfast. ¹¹ To him be the power for ever and ever. Amen.

The Father is saying that "God of all grace, who has called you to His eternal glory in Christ, will restore you after you have endured suffering for a little while will make you strong, firm, and steadfast. His power is eternal. Through your pain, heartache, and hardships, He will bring you through and cancel all enemy attacks. As He makes all things new, you will emerge from the fire unscathed and unchanged by what you've endured. Even if you doubted how or when you would overcome your struggles, the Father is proud of you for not giving up or giving in. You have passed the test, and His strength has carried you through.

MARCH 27ᵀᴴ

Complete Restoration

1 Corinthians 15:10

But by the grace of God, I am what I am, and his grace to me was not without effect. No, I worked harder than all of them—yet not I, but the grace of God that was with me.

Exodus 20:3

"You shall have no other gods before me.

The Father is saying, "Know about His work of restoration in your life." He is restoring your mind, emotions, and heart. This restoration is a result of His special favor and grace. Just as Paul worked diligently, acknowledging that it was God's grace working through him, so is your transformation a reflection of His unmerited favor. As you remove the idols from your life and obey His voice, remember that obedience is greater than sacrifice. Trust in His promise of complete restoration and embrace the truth that He is the only God in your life.

MARCH 28 TH

The Power of Praise

Ephesians 5:27

and to present her to himself as a radiant church, without stain or wrinkle or any other blemish, but holy and blameless.

Romans 8:6

The mind governed by the flesh is death, but the mind governed by the Spirit is life and peace.

The Father is saying that true breakthrough occurs when you lift up praises to His name, which is above every other name. Surrender fully to Him and let the things of this world fade away. Ask the Holy Spirit to remove all carnal and worldly desires from your life. God is preparing to return for a spotless bride—a radiant church without stain or wrinkle, holy and blameless. He is a holy God and calls you to be holy as He is. Approach Him with thanksgiving and offer the praise and worship He deserves. Remember, a mind governed by the flesh leads to death, but a mind governed by the Spirit brings life and peace.

MARCH 29ᵀᴴ

Mountains Moved for You

1 Thessalonians 5:16-18

Rejoice always, ¹⁷ pray continually, ¹⁸ give thanks in all circumstances; for this is God's will for you in Christ Jesus.

The Father is saying that He is working all things out for your good, moving mountains of delay, deceit, and hindrance. Despite the enemy's relentless attacks from every angle of your life, remember that no weapon formed against you will prosper. Though you may have felt like giving up, your perseverance and refusal to succumb to the enemy's tactics have not gone unnoticed. The Father is preparing to bless you both financially and spiritually. You have chosen righteousness, and it will remain with you. Beloved, know that you are deeply loved and cared for. Rejoice always, pray continually, and give thanks in all circumstances, for this is God's will for you in Christ Jesus.

MARCH 30TH

Into Deeper Waters

> Psalm 42:7

Deep calls to deep in the roar of your waterfalls;

all your waves and breakers have swept over me.

> Acts 17:26

From one man, he made all the nations that they should inhabit the whole earth, and he marked out their appointed times in history and the boundaries of their lands.

The Father is saying to let Him break down barriers so He can move powerfully in your life and take you deeper. As you trust Him and reach out for His hand in every aspect of your journey, you will experience breakthroughs in areas you didn't even know needed attention. Trusting Him is like walking on water—you may not see the path ahead, but you can rely on His guidance. Changes will begin to unfold, transforming things you were unaware needed change. Praise His holy name, for He is a mighty God doing great things in your life. He is sending new destiny helpers to assist you with your kingdom assignments, whether writing that book or starting that ministry. Trust that He is orchestrating the perfect timing and places for you. Deep calls to deep; His waves and breakers will surround you with His presence.

MARCH 31ST

Breaking Free from Fear

John 10:14-16

"I am the good shepherd; I know my sheep and my sheep know me— 15 just as the Father knows me and I know the Father—and I lay down my life for the sheep. 16 I have other sheep that are not of this sheep pen. I must bring them also. They, too, will listen to my voice, and there shall be one flock and one shepherd.

Psalm 50:15

and call on me in the day of trouble; I will deliver you, and you will honor me."

The Father is saying that doubt and fear can hinder your walk with Him and limit what He can accomplish in your life. Break free from fear, for He has called you to be bold as a lion. When you humble yourself before Him, He will remove all doubt and fear. He can do far more than you can ask, think, or imagine. As your great Shepherd, He invites you to follow His lead. Unlike a hired hand who abandons the sheep when danger comes, the good Shepherd lays down His life for the sheep. The Father watches over you, protects you from the evil one, and guides you with His deep, personal care. Trust in the good Shepherd, who knows you intimately and lays down His life for you.

APRIL 1ST

A New Season of Restoration

> Exodus 34:14

Do not worship any other God, for the Lord, whose name is Jealous, is a jealous God.

> Jeremiah 30:18

This is what the Lord says: "I will restore the fortunes of Jacob's tents and have compassion on his dwellings; the city will be rebuilt on her ruins, and the palace will stand in its proper place."

The Father is saying that you have entered a new month of fresh beginnings and are entering a new season. Whether you have been enduring a drought or a storm in your finances or family, know that He is breaking every cycle of bondage that has kept you bound. Restoration is coming as He removes all the traps the enemy sets. Remain obedient to His voice and avoid idolizing anything or anyone, for the Lord, whose name is Jealous, is a jealous God. Embrace this new season with faith, knowing He brings renewal and freedom into your life.

April 2ⁿᵈ

Peace in the Midst of Trouble

John 16:33

I have told you these things so that in me you may have peace. In this world, you will have trouble. But take heart! I have overcome the world.

Isaiah 54:5-8

For your Maker is your husband— the Lord Almighty is his name— the Holy One of Israel is your Redeemer; he is called the God of all the earth.⁶ The Lord will call you back as if you were a wife deserted and distressed in spirit— a wife who married young, only to be rejected," says your God.⁷ "For a brief moment, I abandoned you, but with deep compassion, I will bring you back. ⁸ In a surge of anger, I hid my face from you for a moment, but with everlasting kindness, I will have compassion on you," says the Lord your Redeemer.

The Father is saying that He has shared these truths so you can find peace in Him. Though you will face trouble, take heart—He has overcome the world. Beloved, you are in this world but not of it. He is your peace, meeting all your needs—mentally, physically, emotionally, and spiritually. As your Maker, the Lord Almighty, and the Holy One of Israel, your Redeemer, He is the God of all the earth. Despite the devil's attempts to use worldly troubles to trap you, resist him, and he will flee. Command the enemy to depart in His name, and he will obey.

APRIL 3ʳᵈ

Serving with Grace

John 12:26

Whoever serves me must follow me, and where I am, my servant also will be. My Father will honor the one who serves me.

The Father is saying you should serve Him and follow where He leads; where He is, there will also be His servant. If you find serving challenging or encounter obstacles, ask the Holy Spirit to increase grace in those areas of your life. Your requests will be granted, beloved. He will fill you with His grace and mercy and continuously pour His presence upon you. Do not focus on your circumstances; look to Him as your Abba Father. He will rescue you. In every situation, take up the shield of faith to extinguish all the flaming darts of the evil one.

APRIL 4ᵀᴴ

Strength and Protection in the Lord

Luke 10:19

I have given you authority to trample on snakes and scorpions and to overcome all the power of the enemy; nothing will harm you.

Psalm 91:4

He will cover you with his feathers, and under his wings, you will find refuge; his faithfulness will be your shield and rampart.

The Father is saying to refresh and renew your mind as you step toward His will. While you may encounter resistance from the enemy, do not be alarmed; he is already under your feet. Take heart, beloved, for the enemy is defeated. Through Christ Jesus, you have been given power and authority to overcome all the enemy's power. Nothing will harm you—no demon, witchcraft, or evil will touch you. You are covered by His blood and sheltered under His wings. His faithful promises are your armor and protection.

APRIL 5TH

Living a Transformed Life

Galatians 5: 19-21

The acts of the flesh are obvious: sexual immorality, impurity, and debauchery; [20] idolatry and witchcraft; hatred, discord, jealousy, fits of rage, selfish ambition, dissensions, factions[21,] and envy; drunkenness, orgies, and the like. I warn you, as I did before, that those who live like this will not inherit the kingdom of God.

Romans 12:2

Do not conform to the pattern of this world, but be transformed by the renewing of your mind. Then, you will be able to test and approve what God's will is—his good, pleasing, and perfect will.

The Father is saying that the acts of sinful nature are evident: sexual immorality, impurity, sensuality, idolatry, witchcraft, hatred, discord, jealousy, fits of rage, selfish ambition, dissensions, factions, envy, drunkenness, and similar behaviors. As previously warned, those who engage in such acts will not inherit the kingdom of God. Anything that takes priority over me is an idol. Place me first in your life, allowing all you do to glorify me. Do not conform to this world; instead, be transformed by renewing your mind. Trust in me, and as you surrender to my will, you will begin to see the fruit of your transformed life.

April 6th

Entering His Presence

Isaiah 49:16

See, I have engraved you on the palms of my hands; your walls are ever before me.

1 Peter 5:7

Cast all your anxiety on him because he cares for you.

The Father is saying to enter His presence with thanksgiving. Continue to worship and praise, for as you pour out your heart, He will pour into you. In His presence, every wave of anxiety will cease, and intrusive thoughts will disappear. You need not worry, beloved, for everything you need is found in Him. You have peace, love, and wholeness in Him. His love for you is the source of all you have. The Lord upholds you with His righteous right hand and has you engraved in the palm of His hand. Release all your worries and concerns, and rest in His comforting presence.

APRIL 7ᵀᴴ

Trust in Eternal Provision

> 1 John 2:17

The world and its desires pass away, but whoever does the will of God lives forever.

The Father is saying that when you rely solely on Him, He will provide all your needs. However, if you trust the things of this world, you will only find emptiness and dryness. Avoid clinging to worldly possessions or people, for they are temporary and fleeting. The world and its desires pass away, but those who follow God's will receive eternal life. Unlike the temporary offerings of this world, what God provides is everlasting—a land flowing with milk and honey. His love is unfailing, and His presence is constant. Bring your struggles to Him; He will heal and make you whole in His perfect, unending love.

APRIL 8TH

A Call to Disciple and Transform

Matthew 28:19-20

Therefore, go and make disciples of all nations, baptizing them in the name of the Father and of the Son and of the Holy Spirit,[20] and teaching them to obey everything I have commanded you. And surely I am with you always, to the very end of the age."

Acts 2:38

Peter replied, "Repent and be baptized, every one of you, in the name of Jesus Christ for the forgiveness of your sins. And you will receive the gift of the Holy Spirit."

The Father is saying you should go forth and make disciples of all nations. Baptize them in the name of the Father, the Son, and the Holy Spirit, and teach them to follow all He has commanded. Know that He is with you always, even to the end of the age. It is time to repent from your sins and turn to His ways, for His ways are higher and better than ours. The Lord promises victory and calls you to embrace it. As Peter declared, repent and be baptized in the name of Jesus Christ for the forgiveness of your sins, and you will receive the gift of the Holy Spirit.

APRIL 9^(TH)

Guidance Through the Spirit

John 14:26

But the Advocate, the Holy Spirit, whom the Father will send in my name, will teach you all things and will remind you of everything I have said to you.

2 Corinthians 3:16-18

But whenever anyone turns to the Lord, the veil is taken away. [17] Now the Lord is the Spirit, and where the Spirit of the Lord is, there is freedom. [18] And we all, who with unveiled faces contemplate the Lord's glory, are being transformed into his image with ever-increasing glory, which comes from the Lord, who is the Spirit.

The Father is saying that you should rely on His Holy Spirit for guidance and direction. Seek the Spirit's wisdom on your path and the people you should engage with. Use discernment in choosing the right people, places, and things, as some may need your help to align with God's leadership. The Holy Spirit will lead you in all truth and keep you from being deceived by the enemy. As you seek the Lord's ways, you will experience freedom and clarity. Remember, where the Spirit of the Lord is, there is freedom, and with the veil removed, you can see and reflect the glory of the Lord.

APRIL 10TH

Power in Unwavering Faith

Matthew 16:19

I will give you the keys of the kingdom of heaven; whatever you bind on earth will be bound in heaven, and whatever you loose on earth will be loosed in heaven."

The Father is saying that unwavering belief empowers you to achieve the impossible. I can accomplish more than you can imagine or ask for. When distractions, delays, or hindrances arise, recognize them as spiritual attacks and rebuke them in the name of Jesus. Remember, I have given you the keys to the kingdom of heaven; what you bind on earth will be bound in heaven, and what you lose on earth will be loosed in heaven. Through Christ Jesus, you hold power and authority over all the enemy.

APRIL 11TH

Renewal Through the Cross

> ## Luke 23:34-46
>
> ³⁴ Jesus said, "Father, forgive them, for they do not know what they are doing." And they divided up his clothes by casting lots. ³⁵ The people stood watching, and the rulers even sneered at him. They said, "He saved others; let him save himself if he is God's Messiah, the Chosen One." ³⁶ The soldiers also came up and mocked him. They offered him wine vinegar ³⁷ and said, "If you are the king of the Jews, save yourself." ³⁸ There was a written notice above him, which read: this is the king of the Jews. ³⁹ One of the criminals who hung there hurled insults at him: "Aren't you the Messiah? Save yourself and us!" ⁴⁰ But the other criminal rebuked him. "Don't you fear God," he said, "since you are under the same sentence? ⁴¹ We are punished justly, for we are getting what our deeds deserve. But this man has done nothing wrong." ⁴² Then he said, "Jesus, remember me when you come into your kingdom." ⁴³ Jesus answered him, "Truly I tell you, today you will be with me in paradise. ⁴⁴ It was now about noon, and darkness came over the whole land until three in the afternoon, ⁴⁵ for the sun stopped shining. And the curtain of the temple was torn in two. ⁴⁶ Jesus called out with a loud voice, "Father, into your hands I commit my spirit." When he had said this, he breathed his last.

The Father is saying to remember the sacrifice on the cross, where Jesus prayed, "Father, forgive them, for they do not know what they are doing," even as the soldiers gambled for His clothing and a crowd watched. I am the resurrection and the life; those who believe in Me will live. Reflect on the ways I have already brought resurrection into your life. Today, I desire to renew and restore you. I want to refresh your mental health, restore your hope where it has been lost, and revive your faith. I am restoring your ministry and setting things back in order. Embrace all that I have for you by faith in Jesus' name.

APRIL 12TH

A Call to Boldness

Joshua 1:9

Have I not commanded you? Be strong and courageous. Do not be afraid; do not be discouraged, for the Lord your God will be with you wherever you go."

The Father is saying that the days of merely going through the motions are over. The time of glorifying and idolizing men has passed. The Lord now seeks those who stand firm for what is holy and true. We serve a just and righteous God, the King of kings and Lord of Lords. It is time to take a bold stand for the kingdom of God and to fulfill the Great Commission by teaching and preaching the gospel. If the Lord has directed you to act in a certain area and you have hesitated, move today. Stand firm for your Father in heaven and obey His voice. Remember His command: "Be strong and courageous. Do not be afraid or discouraged, for the Lord your God will be with you wherever you go."

APRIL 13ᵀᴴ

Discernment and True Fruit

Matthew 7:15-23

¹⁵ "Watch out for false prophets. They come to you in sheep's clothing, but inwardly, they are ferocious wolves. ¹⁶ By their fruit, you will recognize them. Do people pick grapes from thornbushes or figs from thistles? ¹⁷ Likewise, every good tree bears good fruit, but a bad tree bears bad fruit. ¹⁸ A good tree cannot bear bad fruit, and a bad tree cannot bear good fruit. ¹⁹ Every tree that does not bear good fruit is cut down and thrown into the fire. ²⁰ Thus, by their fruit, you will recognize them. ²¹ "Not everyone who says to me, 'Lord, Lord,' will enter the kingdom of heaven, but only the one who does the will of my Father who is in heaven. ²² Many will say to me on that day, 'Lord, Lord, did we not prophesy in your name and in your name drive out demons and in your name perform many miracles?' ²³ Then I will tell them plainly, 'I never knew you. Away from me, you evildoers!'

Genesis 3:18

It will produce thorns and thistles for you, and you will eat the plants of the field.

The Father is saying to be wary of those who appear righteous but are inwardly ravenous wolves. You will know them by their fruits. Do their actions reflect the fruits of the Spirit—joy, peace, patience, kindness, goodness, gentleness, and self-control? Just as grapes are not gathered from thornbushes, and figs are not picked from thistles, a healthy tree bears good fruit, while a diseased tree bears bad fruit. A healthy tree cannot produce bad fruit, and every tree that does not bear good fruit will be cut down and thrown into the fire. Allow Me to prune and cleanse you, removing anything that does not bear good fruit, in Jesus' name.

APRIL 14^(TH)

Sufficient Grace for Every Need

Ephesians 2:8

For it is by grace you have been saved, through faith—and this is not from yourselves, it is the gift of God—

Romans 5:20-21

The law was brought in so that the trespass might increase. But where sin increased, grace increased all the more, ²¹ so that, just as sin reigned in death, so also grace might reign through righteousness to bring eternal life through Jesus Christ our Lord.

The Father is saying, "My grace is sufficient for you, my beloved. When you face challenges and things seem more complicated than they appear, ask My Holy Spirit for grace." Whether you need help teaching, preaching, or striving to fast, seek My grace in everything you do. My grace is enough for every situation. When relationships at work are difficult or achieving your goals seems out of reach, invite My presence and grace into all you undertake.

If there's someone you need to forgive, ask My Holy Spirit for the grace to extend forgiveness. In My grace, financial lack, addiction, and confusion about your calling will be overcome. I am bringing you clarity and peace that surpasses all understanding. What might have taken others years to accomplish will be achieved more swiftly for you. My grace will make a difference in your life and ministry.

Remember, My grace is for you in trials, tribulations, and testing. You are more than a conqueror in Christ Jesus. Walk in My perfect peace, grace, and mercy each day.

APRIL 15TH

Trusting God in Every Season

Psalm 23:4

Even though I walk through the darkest valley, I will fear no evil, for you are with me; your rod and your staff, they comfort me.

The Father is saying, "Trust Me in the wilderness, for I am the one who fills your cup to overflowing. Trust Me in the valley and count on Me in every circumstance, whether you feel low or high. My joy is your strength, and I am the God of both the valley and the mountaintop." Understand that transformation is necessary. I am working on your character, mind, and heart, removing what no longer serves you and replacing it with fruit that will bear much good in Jesus' name. As a voice calls in the wilderness to prepare the way for the Lord, I am making straight paths in the desert. Trust in My process and embrace the transformation I bring to your life.

APRIL 16ᵀᴴ

Worship Beyond Feelings

> Psalm 55:22

Cast your cares on the Lord, and he will sustain you;

he will never let the righteous be shaken.

The Father is saying, "Worship Me in spirit and truth, regardless of how you feel. Do not be guided by your emotions but by the Spirit of the living God." Bow down before Me and lay all your burdens at the altar. Leave your worries and concerns at My feet, for I never intended for you to carry such weights.

Cast your burdens on Me, and I will sustain you. The righteous will not be moved or falter in Jesus' name. When intrusive thoughts come, seek the Holy Spirit's guidance to discern whether they stem from your flesh or the enemy. Renew your mind by focusing on My Word and My presence. Ask the Holy Spirit to take every thought captive and obey Christ Jesus.

APRIL 17TH

Finding Comfort in His Presence

John 17:23

I in them and you in me—so that they may be brought to complete unity. Then the world will know that you sent me and have loved them even as you have loved me.

The Father is saying, "Let Me wrap My arms around you and envelop you in My presence. I know other things are vying for your attention, but only one truly matters: I, the Lord your God. I will comfort you in times of trouble. When the load feels heavy, cast it upon Me. I care deeply for you and wish to remove your burdens and concerns."

I long to spend time with you, to be united in perfect peace and harmony. Allow Me to fill your cup to overflowing with blessings and joy. My beloved, the battle has already been won. You are in Me, and I am in you. May our unity be so evident that the world will see My love for you and know that I have sent you as I have loved you.

APRIL 18ᵀᴴ

Stepping Out in Faith

Deuteronomy 31:6

Be strong and courageous. Do not be afraid or terrified because of them, for the Lord your God goes with you; he will never leave you nor forsake you."

Joshua 1:9

Have I not commanded you? Be strong and courageous. Do not be afraid; do not be discouraged, for the Lord your God will be with you wherever you go."

The Father is saying, "There are tasks I have asked of you, and your first thoughts might be, 'What if I'm not good enough? What if I make a mistake?' Many of My children walk by sight rather than by faith. I urge you to walk by faith, not by sight." The real question is not about your doubts but whether you will say 'yes' to My call. Show up where I have called you, and I will handle the rest. Show up, and I will speak through you. Show up, and I will move in your life. I will provide the grace you need for the tasks I have set before you. If I have called you to it, trust that I will see you through it. All I ask, my beloved, is for you to step forward in faith, and I will meet you there. Where you fear the most, I will provide abundantly and use you powerfully. Step into what others dream of because of your obedience and trust in Me. You are stepping into a destiny prepared for you, and I will show up in a mighty way. In Jesus' name, show up, and watch Me work wonders through you."

APRIL 19㎢

Letting God Fight Your Battles

> Deuteronomy 30:9

Then the Lord your God will make you most prosperous in all the work of your hands and in the fruit of your womb, the young of your livestock, and the crops of your land. The Lord will again delight in you and make you prosperous, just as he delighted in your ancestors,

> Psalm 90:17

May the favor of the Lord our God rest on us; establish the work of our hands for us— yes, establish the work of our hands.

The Father is saying, "Relax and let Me handle your battles—whether they be in addiction, health, or finances." Command every mountain to be moved in Jesus' name. I assure you that everything you put your hand to will prosper through My name: your health, your ministry, your children, and your finances. Your faith in Me alone has the power to move any obstacle. I am your God and promise to care for you and meet all your needs according to My riches and glory. Continue to trust Me in all that you do, my beloved."

APRIL 20TH

Restoration in Your Marriage

> 1 Corinthians 7:10-11

To the married, I give this command (not I, but the Lord): A wife must not separate from her husband. ¹¹ But if she does, she must remain unmarried or else be reconciled to her husband. And a husband must not divorce his wife.

On April 20, 2023, the Lord gave me a prophetic dream revealing a husband and wife struggling with disagreements and chaos. Despite the tension and despair you may feel in your marriage, know that the hand of God is upon you both. Even in a hopeless situation, there is hope and joy. The Lord brings restoration where there has been sorrow and dryness, offering living water that never runs dry. Trust in Him fully and witness the revival He brings to your marriage. Pray with me:

"Lord, thank You for all You do for me and my family. I repent of my wicked ways and turn to You. Cleanse me and renew my heart. Create in me a new heart. I release my marriage to You and pray for restoration to come forth now in Jesus' name."

APRIL 21ST

Trusting God in the Waiting

Isaiah 55:8-9

"For my thoughts are not your thoughts, neither are your ways my ways," declares the Lord. [9] "As the heavens are higher than the earth, so are my ways higher than your ways and my thoughts than your thoughts.

Psalm 27:1-14

[1] The Lord is my light and my salvation— whom shall I fear? The Lord is the stronghold of my life— of whom shall I be afraid?[2] When the wicked advance against me to devour me, it is my enemies and my foes who will stumble and fall.[3] Though an army besieges me, my heart will not fear; though war break out against me, even then I will be confident.[4] One thing I ask from the Lord, this only do I seek:

That I may dwell in the house of the Lord all the days of my life, to gaze on the beauty of the Lord and to seek him in his temple.[5] For in the day of trouble, he will keep me safe in his dwelling; he will hide me in the shelter of his sacred tent and set me high upon a rock.[6] Then my head will be exalted above the enemies who surround me; at his sacred tent, I will sacrifice with shouts of joy; I will sing and make music to the Lord.[7] Hear my voice when I call, Lord; be merciful to me and answer me. [8] My heart says of you, "Seek his face!" Your face, Lord, I will seek.[9] Do not hide your face from me; do not turn your servant away in anger; you have been my helper. Do not reject me or forsake me, God my Savior.[10] Though my father and mother forsake me, the Lord will receive me.[11] Teach me your way, Lord; lead me in a straight path because of my oppressors.[12] Do not turn me over to the desire of my foes, for false witnesses rise up against me, spouting malicious accusations.[13] I remain confident of this: I will see the goodness of the Lord in the land of the living.[14] Wait for the Lord; be strong and take heart and wait for the Lord.

The Father is saying, "As you wait for me to move in your life, know that I am also waiting on you." Are you ready to confront the fears and anxieties that have held you back? Let go and allow me to remove all fear and anxiety from your life. Be open and honest with me about your feelings, and bring all your burdens before me. I can clear away all obstacles and distractions. Have faith and step into the job or career I have prepared for you. It's okay if you don't understand the path; trust and obedience matter. Remember, my thoughts and ways are higher than yours, just as the heavens are above the earth. Trust in my plans and timing.

APRIL 22ND

Guidance Through Peace

John 4:24

God is spirit, and his worshipers must worship in the Spirit and in truth."

Psalm 27:1

The Lord is my light and my salvation—whom shall I fear? The Lord is the stronghold of my life— of whom shall I be afraid?

The Father is saying, "I will clear the path for you and direct you in the way you should go." You will recognize my guidance through the peace and grace in your life. My righteous right hand sustains you, and my Holy Spirit will lead you. When faced with decisions, seek the Holy Spirit's counsel, and I will confirm your path. I am always with you, desiring to commune with you. Worship me in spirit and truth, and trust in my guidance.

APRIL 23ʳᵈ

Victory in Discouragement

John 6:35

Then Jesus declared, "I am the bread of life. Whoever comes to me will never go hungry, and whoever believes in me will never be thirsty.

Psalm 37:4

Take delight in the Lord, and he will give you the desires of your heart.

The Father is saying, "When you feel discouraged, remember that I, the Lord, win every victory." Rebuke the spirit of self-pity and disappointment, commanding both to be cast away in Jesus' name. Even when life circumstances seem to knock you down, rise up and remember you are a child of God. You have victory no matter how things appear. You are more than a conqueror in Christ Jesus and can do everything through Him who strengthens you. Your dreams and goals are within reach. You are doing well as a mother, wife, husband, or friend because I love you. I see and hear you; you are not overlooked. I will support and strengthen you in all you do because of my love for you. I am your strength.

APRIL 24ᵀᴴ

Faith in Christ Alone

John 6:35

Then Jesus declared, "I am the bread of life. Whoever comes to me will never go hungry, and whoever believes in me will never be thirsty."

Psalm 37:4

Take delight in the Lord, and he will give you the desires of your heart.

The Father is saying, "Place your faith in Me alone, not in the world or its temporary gains." Relying on worldly things will leave you broken, lost, and confused, but in Christ Jesus, you will find true peace and identity. Many seek love in the wrong places—through drugs, alcohol, or people—but these will ultimately fail and leave you feeling hopeless. In Me, you will discover genuine peace and love. You will no longer thirst, hunger, or beg for anything; the Lord will provide all your needs. In Me, you will find everything your heart desires.

APRIL 25ᵀᴴ

Guided by the Shepherd

> Psalm 23:24

Even though I walk through the darkest valley, I will fear no evil, for you are with me; your rod and your staff, they comfort me.

The Father is saying, be steadfast in your journey, avoiding both haste and delay. Let the Holy Spirit guide your steps. As your Great Shepherd, I call you by name, and you will know the path. I lead you to green pastures and beside still waters. If you encounter confusion or delays, rebuke those demonic forces and cancel their influence in the name of Jesus. Keep your focus on Me, setting your heart and mind on things above, where Christ is seated at the right hand of God. Remember, your life is now hidden with Christ in God.

APRIL 26ᵀᴴ

Renewed Strength in Every Challenge

> Psalm 73:26

My flesh and my heart may fail, but God is the strength of my heart and my portion forever.

> Ezekiel 36:27

And I will put my Spirit in you and move you to follow my decrees and be careful to keep my laws.

The Father is saying when you feel depleted in your job, family, or ministry, ask the Holy Spirit to refresh you from head to toe. Come to Me for rest and drink from the living water I offer. I will renew your strength and fill you to overflowing. Though your flesh may be weak, My Spirit is strong within you. I am giving you the extra push needed to overcome challenges, complete tasks, and achieve goals. I am present in your ministry, ready to be praised and worshipped with thanksgiving. Thank Me for all I have done and what I am about to do. I am stepping into every problem and situation, including financial struggles and battles. It is already done in Jesus' name.

APRIL 27ᵀᴴ

Trusting God with Tomorrow

Philippians 4:6

Do not be anxious about anything, but in every situation, by prayer and petition, with thanksgiving, present your requests to God.

Matthew 6:34

Therefore do not worry about tomorrow, for tomorrow will worry about itself. Each day has enough trouble of its own.

The Father is saying, "Don't worry about tomorrow; each day has enough trouble." Whether you're concerned about how a job situation will resolve, the outcome of a meeting, a doctor's report, or a family member's salvation, remember that it's not your job to understand everything but to trust Me. I am in control of every situation you face. Every care and concern is in My hands. Release your worries, and let Me guide you through this path. Your flesh may lead you astray, but My Spirit will guide you faithfully. My strength is made perfect in your weakness. Trust in Me and let My Spirit lead you.

APRIL 28ᵀᴴ

Embracing the Process

1 Peter 4:12-13

Dear friends, do not be surprised at the fiery ordeal that has come on you to test you, as though something strange were happening to you. ¹³ But rejoice inasmuch as you participate in the sufferings of Christ, so that you may be overjoyed when his glory is revealed.

The Father is saying that this process is essential for your growth; it is a time of purification and sanctification. I am calling you to a higher purpose that others may not understand. Some may even envy the anointing I have placed on your life. Pray for them, as they do not know what they are doing. I have designed you for this moment. The refining fire you feel inside is part of the transformation I am working on in you. It may be hard to put into words or understand, but you are not meant to comprehend everything. My grace is sufficient for you, and My peace is with you. I am elevating you to a new dimension, and while you may wish to bring others along, this journey is uniquely yours. Seek My Holy Spirit for discernment and grace as you follow My perfect will for your life.

APRIL 29ᵀᴴ

Finding Strength in My Presence

Colossians 1:11

being strengthened with all power according to his glorious might so that you may have great endurance and patience

Acts 1:8

But you will receive power when the Holy Spirit comes on you, and you will be my witnesses in Jerusalem, and in all Judea and Samaria, and to the ends of the earth."

The Father is saying that as you immerse yourself in My presence, I will fill you with My Spirit. My Spirit dwells within you, and together, we can navigate every challenge, even the small tasks like cleaning the house or washing the dishes. I care about every detail of your life and want to be present in all that you do. Remember, you never face anything alone. I empower you to be greater and achieve more. Surrender to My will, ignore distractions, and rebuke them in Jesus' name. With My presence, we can overcome anything together.

APRIL 30ᵀᴴ

Claiming Victory in Jesus' Name

Deuteronomy 20:4

For the Lord your God is the one who goes with you to fight for you against your enemies to give you victory."

The Father is saying, "When defeat whispers your name, call on My name, Jesus." "Victory is yours—victory in your marriage, career, and every area of your life because of the blood of Jesus. The Lord, your God, goes with you to fight against your enemies and grant you victory. It doesn't matter what challenges come your way; by faith in My name, the name above every other name, you claim victory. Trust that I will win every battle for you. Victory belongs to you, My beloved.

MAY 1ST

Strength in Trials

> **2 Corinthians 4:8**

We are hard pressed on every side, but not crushed, perplexed, but not in despair;

The Father is saying, "Although you may face many trials and persecutions from all directions, I am with you and will provide the strength you need." Fix your eyes on Me alone when you feel surrounded and overwhelmed. Meet Me in the secret place where I dwell among you. I will equip you to endure the trials you face. Though you may feel confused and unable to understand your situation fully, you will look back a year from now and see how much you have grown in spirit and strength. You will never face anything alone. I am upholding you, and I am proud of you!

MAY 2ND

Bearing Fruit Through the Holy Spirit

Zechariah 4:6

So he said to me, "This is the word of the Lord to Zerubbabel:'Not by might nor by power, but by my Spirit,' says the Lord Almighty.

John 13:35

By this, everyone will know that you are my disciples if you love one another."

The Father is saying that the Holy Spirit will help you bear fruit, so there's no need to rush or feel pressured to produce results immediately. Your journey with Me is a process of growth and transformation. You will bear much fruit as you walk in humility and trust in My power within you. The Holy Spirit works in you, refining your character by removing sinful traits and replacing them with godly qualities. This transformation will reveal My glory to the world and others, demonstrating that I am alive and dwell within you. Remember, it's not by might or power but by the Spirit of God that you bear fruit and walk in the fullness of His power. Declare this as a prophetic act: "I am bearing the fruits of the Spirit—love, joy, peace, patience, goodness, gentleness, kindness, and self-control—in the mighty name of Jesus."

MAY 3RD

Step Into Your Assignment

Hebrews 11:6

And without faith, it is impossible to please God, because anyone who comes to him must believe that he exists and that he rewards those who earnestly seek him.

Job 33:4

The Spirit of God has made me; the breath of the Almighty gives me life.

The Father is saying, "Take charge of the assignment I have given you." Whether it's writing that book revealed to you in a dream or vision or starting that business, this is your confirmation to begin now. Whether serving in your church or starting a ministry, do it with faith and obedience. I will provide for you financially, mentally, and emotionally. Remember, you act by faith, for without faith, it is impossible to please Me. I am with you, and I will provide the words you need. Show up, and I will show up. As a child of the Most High God, trust that My hand is on your endeavor. Move forward and watch Me breathe life into your work.

MAY 4ᵀᴴ

Faith in the Impossible

> 2 Corinthians 5:17

Therefore, if anyone is in Christ, the new creation has come:[a] The old has gone, the new is here!

The Father is saying, "When you believe with all your heart, mind, and soul, you can do all things through Me." It doesn't matter what you see or hear; I can do everything through and within you. Today, lay down all unbelief and doubt. Take up your cross and follow Me with unwavering faith. Do not place your trust in man but in Me alone. Bow only to Me and rebuke every lie from the enemy. Ask My Holy Spirit to align your mind with Christ Jesus. I am making all things new in your life. Embrace the renewal and see the impossible become possible in Jesus' name.

MAY 5™

Trust in My Perfect Timing

> 1 Peter 5:6-7

Humble yourselves, therefore, under God's mighty hand, that he may lift you up in due time. ⁷ Cast all your anxiety on him because he cares for you.

> 2 Peter 3:8

But do not forget this one thing, dear friends: With the Lord, a day is like a thousand years, and a thousand years are like a day.

The Father is saying, "Do not give up or succumb to the enemy's tactics." You may feel discouraged because things are not unfolding as you expected or moving according to your timeline. Remember, everything is under My control, and My timing is always perfect. I hold the entire world in My hands and am the great I AM. Everything I do is in perfect timing.

Whether you are waiting for a job promotion, a doctor's report, or going through a refining process, know that these moments are meant to strengthen your faith and reaffirm that I am God. I am the Refiner, and everything is within My perfect will for your life. Release your discouragement to Me and surrender everything to My care. Wait and see the outcome when I am in control.

MAY 6TH

Finding Strength in Your ABBA

Isaiah 59:1

Surely the arm of the Lord is not too short to save, nor his ear too dull to hear.

The Father saying that when life becomes challenging, remember you have an ABBA who fights for you with unmatched fervor. I am all you need. Many of My children expend energy on matters that ultimately do not matter. In moments of hopelessness, remember that I am your hope and salvation. Find rest in Me. Bring all your cares and concerns to Me, for I am attentive to every word you speak. The arm of the Lord is never too short to save, nor is His ear too dull to hear.

MAY 7ᵀᴴ

Trusting in Divine Care

Job 11:18

You will be secure, because there is hope; you will look about you and take your rest in safety.

Psalm 122:6-7

Pray for the peace of Jerusalem: "May those who love you be secure. ⁷ May there be peace within your walls and security within your citadels."

The Father is saying that as you lean in and trust Me with all your heart, soul, and mind, you will find greater peace. It may feel like I am taking things away, but I only remove what cannot stay. Everything that is not of Me must go because you are My beloved. I know what is best for you and have you safely in My hand. I am teaching you to trust Me fully. You are always secure in My care; even death cannot breach your safety in Christ. You will find hope and rest as you experience My protection.

MAY 8TH

The Power of Sacrificial Praise

> Psalm 50:14

"Sacrifice thank offerings to God, fulfill your vows to the Most High,

The Father is saying, "Bring Me the sacrifice of your praise." As you lift your voice in gratitude and worship, you open the gates of heaven and invite My presence into your life. I am always with you—surrounding, guiding, and knowing every detail of your life. There is nothing about you that I do not see or understand. Even in your trials, you are never alone; I care for everything. Praise and worship are powerful; they make demons flee, cause shifts in your circumstances, and bring about breakthroughs. Every chain that binds you will break in Jesus' name in your worship. Worship Me.

MAY 9TH

Guard Your Heart and Mind

> Luke 21:34-36

"Be careful, or your hearts will be weighed down with carousing, drunkenness, and the anxieties of life, and that day will close on you suddenly like a trap. ³⁵ For it will come on all those who live on the face of the whole earth. ³⁶ Be always on the watch, and pray that you may be able to escape all that is about to happen and that you may be able to stand before the Son of Man."

The Father is saying to be vigilant and avoid letting your heart become burdened by excess or anxiety. Carousing, drunkenness, and the worries of life can ensnare you unexpectedly, like a trap set for those who live without awareness. Stay alert, pray for the strength to escape the challenges ahead, and stand confidently before the Son of Man. Your life should reflect a difference from the world's patterns. Let go of anything that hinders your walk with Me, and allow My Spirit to fill you. Release all anxiety and discouragement into My hands, asking for grace in every area of your life. Do not let the enemy overpower you. Remember who you are in Christ Jesus. I am with you and for you. Take every thought captive and make it obedient to Christ Jesus.

MAY 10TH

Unshakable Foundation

Matthew 5:14

"You are the light of the world. A town built on a hill cannot be hidden.

The Father is saying you will not be moved or shaken; the foundation on which you stand is firm and solid. I have placed you where your enemies cannot reach and adversaries cannot swim. You are the world's light, a city on a hill that cannot be hidden. If you feel you're barely staying afloat, know I am leading you out of the wilderness, delays, and hindrances. I am removing barriers and breaking down walls. With all power and authority in My hands, I call you to be faithful and to serve Me with all your heart, mind, and soul. Receive all that I have for you by faith in Jesus' name.

MAY 11TH

Endurance Through Grace

Galatians 6:9

Let us not become weary in doing good, for at the proper time we will reap a harvest if we do not give up.

Psalm 62:5-12

Yes, my soul, find rest in God; my hope comes from him. ⁶ Truly he is my rock and my salvation; he is my fortress; I will not be shaken.⁷ My salvation and my honor depend on God; he is my mighty rock, my refuge.⁸ Trust in him at all times, you people; pour out your hearts to him, for God is our refuge. Surely the lowborn are but a breath; the highborn are but a lie. If weighed on a balance, they are nothing; together, they are only a breath.¹⁰ Do not trust in extortion or put vain hope in stolen goods; though your riches increase, do not set your heart on them.¹¹ One thing God has spoken, two things I have heard: "Power belongs to you, God,¹² and with you, Lord, is unfailing love"; and, "You reward everyone according to what they have done."

The Father is saying to persevere through these challenging times and trials. Do not grow weary of doing good, for in due season, you will reap if you do not give up. You need endurance to do the will of God and receive what is promised. Remember, the one who endures to the end will be saved. As you press on and move forward, you will find My grace pushing you, giving you strength where you feel weak. My grace is sufficient for you; I am all that you need. Everything you desire, want, and need is found in Me alone.

MAY 12TH

Release and Trust

Psalm 34:7

The angel of the Lord encamps around those who fear him, and he delivers them.

The Father is saying it's time to unwind from everything you're feeling and release it to Me. Seek My face and align your heart with Mine, for those desires will also become yours. Trust Me with the issues you're dealing with, whether it's a situation with your child, your marriage, or any other concern. You never face any problem alone. I am backing you up. The angel of the Lord encamps around those who fear Him and delivers them. No matter what you're facing, I am with you—behind, beside, and all around you. My beloved, lay it all down today.

MAY 13ᵀᴴ

Abide in Me

John 15:4-11

Remain in me, as I also remain in you. No branch can bear fruit by itself; it must remain in the vine. Neither can you bear fruit unless you remain in me.⁵ "I am the vine; you are the branches. If you remain in me and I in you, you will bear much fruit; apart from me, you can do nothing.⁶ If you do not remain in me, you are like a branch that is thrown away and withers; such branches are picked up, thrown into the fire, and burned. ⁷ If you remain in me and my words remain in you, ask whatever you wish, and it will be done for you. ⁸ This is to my Father's glory that you bear much fruit, showing yourselves to be my disciples.⁹ "As the Father has loved me, so have I loved you. Now remain in my love. ¹⁰ If you keep my commands, you will remain in my love, just as I have kept my Father's commands and remain in his love.¹¹ I have told you this so that my joy may be in you and that your joy may be complete.

The Father is saying that as you wait quietly in My presence, My presence fills that space. My Holy Spirit dwells within you, guiding and teaching you My ways. I am teaching you to trust and abide in Me as I abide in you. Just as a branch cannot bear fruit on its own unless it remains connected to the vine, neither can you bear fruit unless you remain in Me. I am the vine; you are the branches. Those who abide in Me and I in them will bear much fruit. I desire you to bear the fruits of the Spirit: love, peace, joy, patience, kindness, gentleness, goodness, and self-control.

MAY 14TH

Beyond Human Limits

> Deuteronomy 15:6

For the Lord your God will bless you as he has promised, and you will lend to many nations but will borrow from none. You will rule over many nations, but none will rule over you.

The Father is saying that some of My children try to confine Me to their understanding, but I cannot be boxed in. I am God, the Great I AM. Your human mind cannot fully grasp My ways or comprehend My plans. My Word declares that without faith, it is impossible to please Me. Everything you do and say should be rooted in faith in Me alone. Many of you focus on merely getting by, from paycheck to paycheck, but I have greater blessings in store. I want to bless you abundantly so that you can bless others. As I promised, you will lend to many nations but borrow from none and have dominion without being ruled.

MAY 15th

Unveiling Divine Treasures

> Isaiah 45:30

And the LORD shall cause his glorious voice to be heard and shall shew the lighting down of his arm, with the indignation of his anger, and with the flame of a devouring fire, with scattering, and tempest, and hailstones.

The Father is saying that as you journey with Me, I will reveal treasures and riches stored in secret places, so you may know that I am the Lord, the God of Israel, who calls you by name. These treasures require faith in Me alone, a quiet trust that I am God. I am unveiling things to you in ways unseen and unheard by others. When you face doubts and opposition, remember who has spoken to you. It is I, the Lord, who has sent and ordained you.

MAY 16TH

Unshakeable Strength

Psalm 46:7

The Lord Almighty is with us; the God of Jacob is our fortress.

The Father is saying I am the Lord of hosts, and the God of Jacob is your stronghold. No problem is too great for Me, and no circumstance beyond My power to change instantly. Because the Holy Spirit dwells within you, you can access the same power that raised Jesus from the dead. Speak to the mountains of despair and stagnation in your life and command them to move in Jesus' name. Remember, rich in mercy and great love, God has made you alive with Christ, even when you were dead in your trespasses.

MAY 17TH

Standing Firm in the Battle

> Ephesians 6:10-17

Finally, be strong in the Lord and in his mighty power. ¹¹ Put on the full armor of God so that you can take your stand against the devil's schemes. ¹² For our struggle is not against flesh and blood, but against the rulers, against the authorities, against the powers of this dark world and against the spiritual forces of evil in the heavenly realms. ¹³ Therefore put on the full armor of God, so that when the day of evil comes, you may be able to stand your ground, and after you have done everything, to stand. ¹⁴ Stand firm then, with the belt of truth buckled around your waist, with the breastplate of righteousness in place, ¹⁵ and with your feet fitted with the readiness that comes from the gospel of peace. ¹⁶ In addition to all this, take up the shield of faith, with which you can extinguish all the flaming arrows of the evil one. ¹⁷ Take the helmet of salvation and the sword of the Spirit, which is the word of God.

The Father is saying when you face challenges and the enemy attacks you from every direction—whether in your marriage, family, ministry, or finances—submit to Me and resist the enemy. He will flee in Jesus' name. Plead the blood of Jesus and ask the Holy Spirit to send warring angels to combat the rulers, authorities, and powers of this dark world, as well as the spiritual forces of evil in the heavenly realms. You hold full authority over these evil forces. Be strong in the Lord and His mighty power, and put on the full armor of God to stand against the devil's schemes. Remember, our struggle is not against flesh and blood but against the powers of darkness and spiritual forces of evil. Stand firm in your faith in

Christ Jesus alone. The battle is not yours; it is Mine, says the Lord your God.

MAY 18ᵀᴴ

Embracing Humility and Unity

Matthew 18:4

Therefore, whoever takes the lowly position of this child is the greatest in the kingdom of heaven.

Ephesians 4:2-8

Be completely humble and gentle; be patient, bearing with one another in love. ³ Make every effort to keep the unity of the Spirit through the bond of peace. ⁴ There is one body and one Spirit, just as you were called to one hope when you were called; ⁵ one Lord, one faith, one baptism; ⁶ one God and Father of all, who is over all and through all and in all.⁷ But to each one of us grace has been given as Christ apportioned it. ⁸ This is why it says: "When he ascended on high, he took many captives and gave gifts to his people."

The Father is saying, "Be completely humble and gentle in all you do and say. As My children, you represent Me wherever you go." I have called you to humility, for whoever humbles himself like a little child is the greatest in the kingdom of heaven. Be patient and bear with one another in love. Make every effort to maintain the unity of the Spirit through the bond of peace. Strive to be at peace with your brothers and sisters. Truly, whoever hears My word and believes in the One who sent Me has eternal life. There is one body and one Spirit, just as you were called to one hope. There is one Lord, one faith, one baptism, and one God and Father of all, who is over all and through all and in all.

MAY 19TH

Unchanging in a Changing World

Isaiah 44:6

"This is what the Lord says— Israel's King and Redeemer, the Lord Almighty: I am the first, and I am the last; apart from me, there is no God.

Acts 15:16

"'After this, I will return and rebuild David's fallen tent. Its ruins I will rebuild, and I will restore it,

The Father is saying, "Do not be troubled by life's circumstances." People and situations may change, but I remain the same. I am the same yesterday, today, and forever. I am rebuilding your life from the ground up, transforming you in ways that will be evident to those around you. When others see you and hear you speak, they will recognize the power of the living God you serve. I am the Lord, the King of Israel, and your Redeemer, the Lord of hosts. I am the First and the Last; there is no God besides Me. Continue to seek Me and ask My Holy Spirit to teach you My ways. I am proud of you, My beloved.

MAY 20ᵀᴴ

The Call to Obedience

Job 22:21-25

"Submit to God and be at peace with him; in this way, prosperity will come to you. ²² Accept instruction from his mouth and lay up his words in your heart. ²³ If you return to the Almighty, you will be restored: If you remove wickedness far from your tent ²⁴ and assign your nuggets to the dust, your gold of Ophir to the rocks in the ravines, ²⁵ then the Almighty will be your gold, the choicest silver for you.

Deuteronomy 11:22

If you carefully observe all these commands I am giving you to follow—to love the Lord your God, to walk in obedience to him, and to hold fast to him—

The Father is saying that obedience is more significant than sacrifice. I desire for you to be holy and to follow all My commandments. I call you to love one another, even your enemies. If you struggle with obedience, ask My Holy Spirit to reveal what you need to submit or what you may be neglecting. Rebellion is a form of witchcraft and can separate you from My will. If you recognize rebellion in your heart, it's time to repent. Seek My Holy Spirit's grace for the areas you need most. Submit to Me, resist the enemy, and he will flee from you in Jesus' name. Be diligent to follow all My commandments, My beloved.

MAY 21ST

Remaining in My Love

John 15:18-27

"If the world hates you, keep in mind that it hated me first. [19] If you belonged to the world, it would love you as its own. As it is, you do not belong to the world, but I have chosen you out of the world. That is why the world hates you. [20] Remember what I told you: 'A servant is not greater than his master.' If they persecuted me, they will persecute you also. If they obeyed my teaching, they will obey yours also. [21] They will treat you this way because of my name, for they do not know the one who sent me. [22] If I had not come and spoken to them, they would not be guilty of sin, but now they have no excuse for their sin. [23] Whoever hates me hates my Father as well. [24] If I had not done among them the works no one else did, they would not be guilty of sin. As it is, they have seen, and yet they have hated both me and my Father. [25] But this is to fulfill what is written in their Law: 'They hated me without reason.' [26] "When the Advocate comes, whom I will send to you from the Father—the Spirit of truth who goes out from the Father—he will testify about me. [27] And you also must testify, for you have been with me from the beginning.

The Father is saying, "By obeying My commands, you will remain in My love, just as I have obeyed My Father's commands and remain in His love." You are safe and secure in My hands, My beloved. Though you face many trials and hardships, consider it joy when you encounter various trials, for testing your faith produces patience. Let patience have its perfect work so that you may be complete, lacking nothing. Remember, they did it to me first when you were gossiped about, cursed, or slandered.

The world would love you if you belonged to it, but you are not of this world; therefore, the world may hate you, but I love you deeply.

MAY 22ND

Finding Rest in Surrender

> James 4:7

Submit yourselves, then, to God. Resist the devil, and he will flee from you.

> Matthew 11:28

"Come to me, all you who are weary and burdened, and I will give you rest.

The Father is saying, "Come to Me, all you who are weary and burdened, and I will give you rest." Bring your concerns and worries to Me, including those things, people, or situations that trouble you most. These are the areas where your trust in Me might be lacking. Surrender them at My feet and focus on worshiping Me. Do not be distracted by the attacks or look to the left or the right. If you are experiencing intense warfare in your mind and heart, redirect your focus to Me. In your submission and obedience, you will see the enemy flee in Jesus' name.

MAY 23ʳᵈ

Victory in the Roar

> Ephesians 6:12

For our struggle is not against flesh and blood but against the rulers, against the authorities, against the powers of this dark world, and against the spiritual forces of evil in the heavenly realms.

The Father is saying, "When the adversary attacks like a roaring lion, stand firm and remember that the Lion of Judah is within you." Do not be discouraged. The Lion of the tribe of Judah, the root of David, has conquered all, making it possible to open the scroll and its seven seals. You have victory over every attack. The weapons of our warfare are not carnal but mighty through God for pulling down strongholds. We fight not against flesh and blood but against principalities, powers, rulers of darkness, and spiritual forces of evil in the heavenly realms.

MAY 24ᵀᴴ

Eternal Perspective

Joshua 1:9

Have I not commanded you? Be strong and courageous. Do not be afraid; do not be discouraged, for the Lord your God will be with you wherever you go."

The Father is saying that the challenges you face now are nothing compared to the eternity awaiting you in heaven. Your struggles are not in vain. Let not your hearts be troubled; trust in God and me. In my Father's house, there are many rooms. If it were not so, I would have told you that I go to prepare a place for you. I will come again and take you to myself so that where I am, you may be also. Stay close to me in the secret place, immersed in my word and fully submitted to my will. If you encounter obstacles, ask the Holy Spirit for grace to overcome every attack on your mind and emotions and to dispel all doubt. Have I not commanded you? Be strong and courageous; do not be afraid or discouraged, for the Lord your God will be with you wherever you go.

MAY 25TH

Exalting the Lord

> 1 Peter 5:6-7

Humble yourselves, therefore, under God's mighty hand, that he may lift you up in due time. ⁷ Cast all your anxiety on him because he cares for you.

The Father is saying, "Exalt my holy name. Lift me up, for I am your LORD GOD, your rescuer and deliverer. I can restore you and bring order to your life. As the King of Kings and Lord of Lords, I am capable of more than you can think, ask, or imagine." It will be given to you when you ask anything in my name. If you have not received it, it may be because your motives do not align with my will. Ensure that your heart posture is right when you ask, humbling yourself under the mighty hand of God so that at the proper time, He may lift you up. Cast all your anxieties on Him, for He cares for you.

MAY 26TH

Trust in My Plan

Isaiah 40:28

Do you not know? Have you not heard? The Lord is the everlasting God, the Creator of the ends of the earth. He will not grow tired or weary, and his understanding no one can fathom.

Isaiah 55:8

"For my thoughts are not your thoughts, neither are your ways my ways," declares the Lord.

The Father is saying, "Do not doubt what I can do in you and through you, my beloved." Your mind cannot fully grasp what I am accomplishing in your life. I ask that you hold my hand never let go, and follow my commandments. I am the author and finisher of your faith, who endured the cross for the joy set before Him, despising the shame, and now sits at the right hand of God. I know the beginning and the end, for I am both. I am always moving and working behind the scenes in your life. You are secure in the palm of my hand. My thoughts and ways are higher than yours, declares the Lord. I am teaching you to walk in truth and to rely on me.

MAY 27TH

Embrace the Day with Gratitude

Luke 22:42

"Father, if you are willing, take this cup from me; yet not my will, but yours be done."

Philippians 1:3-11

I thank my God every time I remember you. [4] In all my prayers for all of you, I always pray with joy [5] because of your partnership in the gospel from the first day until now, [6] being confident of this, that he who began a good work in you will carry it on to completion until the day of Christ Jesus.

[7] It is right for me to feel this way about all of you since I have you in my heart, and whether I am in chains or defending and confirming the gospel, all of you share in God's grace with me. [8] God can testify how I long for all of you with the affection of Christ Jesus.

[9] And this is my prayer: that your love may abound more and more in knowledge and depth of insight, [10] so that you may be able to discern what is best and may be pure and blameless for the day of Christ, [11] filled with the fruit of righteousness that comes through Jesus Christ—to the glory and praise of God.

The Father is saying, "Rejoice and be glad, for this is the day the Lord has made!" When unexpected events arise, don't let frustration take hold. Instead, whisper, "Thank you, Jesus, for all you do." I am teaching you the essence of gratitude. Give thanks in every circumstance, whether good or bad. I am constantly at work, orchestrating everything for your benefit.

Renew your mind daily with the Word of God and remain attentive to My voice. Remove distractions and ask the Holy Spirit to guide you, seeking not your will but Mine, in Jesus' name.

MAY 28ᵀᴴ

Unleash Your Gifts

Psalm 91:11

For he will command his angels concerning you to guard you in all your ways;

The Father is saying, "It's time to push forward with the gifts I have placed within you." This is the moment to bring forth every talent and calling I have entrusted you. You are a force to be reckoned with, and no devil or person can hinder what I have set in motion. Keep moving forward, pressing on, and running this race with unwavering faith. I am with you, and My grace has increased in your life. Do not wait on man; I am God. My hand is upon you, and every gift I have given you is coming to fruition. I have commissioned angels to go before, beside, and around you. Do not doubt what I have placed inside you.

MAY 29TH

Stay Focused and Unwavering

Isaiah 41:13

For I am the Lord your God who takes hold of your right hand and says to you, Do not fear; I will help you.

1 Corinthians 14:33

For God is not a God of disorder but of peace—as in all the congregations of the Lord's people.

The Father is saying, "Do not let the enemy distract or deceive you." Rebuke every plot and scheme in the name of Jesus, for we are not unaware of his tactics. The enemy may bring confusion and discouragement, but look to Me as your help and refuge. Reject every thought from the enemy and take every thought captive, making it obedient to Christ Jesus. Be encouraged, child of God; I am with you wherever you go.

MAY 30ᵀᴴ

Remain on the Narrow Path

Isaiah 64:8

Yet you, Lord, are our Father. We are the clay, you are the potter; we are all the work of your hand.

Proverbs 4:18

The path of the righteous is like the morning sun, shining ever brighter till the full light of day.

Matthew 7:14

But small is the gate and narrow the road that leads to life, and only a few find it.

The Father is saying that you should continue on the narrow path you have chosen. You are on the right path, and you need not worry. Many have questioned if they follow the Lord's call, let go of all doubt, and ask, "Lord, consume me. All I want is You." Allow My presence to work through you and in you. Testing and pruning are part of this journey, removing what is not of Me. Trust that My will is being done in your life. Though you face challenges and anxieties, My grace is sufficient. Decide today to trust Me completely. Ask the Holy Spirit to release grace if you struggle with your concerns. Remember, I am the potter, and you are the clay. You are in the palm of My hand. You are Mine, and I am yours.

MAY 31ST

Faithful Through Trials

1 Timothy 1:18

Timothy, my son, I am giving you this command in keeping with the prophecies once made about you so that by recalling them, you may fight the battle well,

Psalm 18:34

He trains my hands for battle; my arms can bend a bow of bronze.

2 Corinthians 10:3

For though we live in the world, we do not wage war as the world does.

The Father is saying, "Remain faithful to Me through every trial, test, battle, and moment of warfare." Count it all joy when you face various trials, for they produce perseverance and confirm your trust in Me. This process is vital for your growth. Know that these trials strengthen you and prepare you to mature and lack nothing. Even when you feel weary amid warfare, remember I am with you, providing strength and support. I am fighting for you and cheering you on every step of the way. You will overcome because I am with you, and you have victory over all the enemy's powers.

JUNE 1ST

Unfailing Love in Every Circumstance

Isaiah 54:10

Though the mountains be shaken and the hills be removed,

yet my unfailing love for you will not be shaken, nor my covenant of peace is removed," says the Lord, who has compassion on you.

Psalm 136:26

Give thanks to the God of heaven. *His love endures forever.*

Psalm 86:15

But you, Lord, are a compassionate and gracious God, slow to anger, abounding in love and faithfulness.

The Father is saying, "When everything seems to fall apart, remember that My love for you never fails." Whether things are not going as planned, your children are not listening, or the tasks seem overwhelming, My love remains constant and unwavering. You are precious to Me and close to My heart. I am here to help you with each challenge you face. I know we will get through it together as you focus on me. Begin this month with the expectation of sudden change, for I am actively working all things out for your good. Even if mountains shake and hills are removed, My unfailing love and covenant of peace will remain steadfast.

JUNE 2ND

Focus on My Perfection

> Jeremiah 1:5
>
> "Before I formed you in the womb I knew[a] you,
>
> before you were born I set you apart;
>
> I appointed you as a prophet to the nations."

> Psalm 46:10
>
> He says, "Be still, and know that I am God;
>
> I will be exalted among the nations,
>
> I will be exalted in the earth."

The Father is saying, "Begin by worshiping and praising My holy name." I am Jehovah Rapha, Elohim, the great I AM. Praise the Lord your God, for I will be exalted among the nations and the earth. Be still and know that I AM GOD. Instead of striving for perfection in everything you do, focus on My perfect love for you. You do not need to be perfect—do your best with a spirit of excellence in the tasks I have given you. All I ask is for you to show up; I will handle the rest. Remember, I knew you before I formed you in the womb; I sanctified and ordained you for My purposes before you were born.

JUNE 3ᴿᴰ

Fear Is Not Your Portion

Philippians 4:19

And my God will meet all your needs according to the riches of his glory in Christ Jesus.

The Father is saying that fear is not your portion; it is a liar and a thief. While the enemy comes to steal, kill, and destroy, I have come to give you life and life more abundantly. My power resides within you. Have I not commanded you to be strong and courageous? Do not let fear take hold, for I am the Lord your God. I will strengthen, help, and uphold you with My righteous right hand. Though we live in this world, our battles are not fought similarly. You will receive everything you need or ask in My name, according to My riches and glory, by faith.

JUNE 4TH

Guarding Your Thoughts

Ephesians 6:13

Therefore, put on the full armor of God so that when the day of evil comes, you may be able to stand your ground and after you have done everything, to stand.

2 Corinthians 10:5

We demolish arguments and every pretension that sets itself up against the knowledge of God, and we take captive every thought to make it obedient to Christ.

The Father is saying, "Not all thoughts are from Me." Some thoughts entering your mind may come from the enemy. When you receive such thoughts, ask the Holy Spirit to help you discern their source. Recognize and rebuke any lies from the adversary, casting them back to the abyss. Immediately take these thoughts captive and make them obedient to Christ Jesus. When attacks on your mind arise, stand firm by putting on the full armor of God. Use the shield of faith to extinguish all the flaming arrows of the evil one.

JUNE 5ᵀᴴ

Victory in Christ

Romans 8:17

Now, if we are children, then we are heirs—heirs of God and co-heirs with Christ, if indeed we share in his sufferings in order that we may also share in his glory.

Luke 10:19

I have given you authority to trample on snakes and scorpions and to overcome all the power of the enemy; nothing will harm you.

The Father is saying, do not doubt what I am doing in your life. You are not defeated despite the attacks on your mind and spiritual life. You are more than a conqueror in Christ Jesus, who loves you. Remember yourself and your true identity during hardships and struggles—you are a child of the Most High God. I am with you, as I raised us from the dead with Christ and seated us in the heavenly realms because of our union with Him. Though you may face mental, physical, and financial attacks, these are permitted for My glory. Remember, as children and heirs of God, joint heirs with Christ, we will share in His sufferings and glory. Stand firm, knowing you have victory over every demonic attack and all enemy power.

JUNE 6ᵀᴴ

Set Your Heart on Heaven

Colossians 3:1-4

Since, then, you have been raised with Christ, set your hearts on things above, where Christ is, seated at the right hand of God.² Set your minds on things above, not on earthly things. ³ For you died, and your life is now hidden with Christ in God. ⁴ When Christ, who is your[a] life, appears, then you also will appear with him in glory.

James 4:7-10

Submit yourselves, then, to God. Resist the devil, and he will flee from you. ⁸ Come near to God, and he will come near to you. Wash your hands, you sinners, and purify your hearts, you double-minded. ⁹ Grieve, mourn, and wail. Change your laughter to mourning and your joy to gloom. ¹⁰ Humble yourselves before the Lord, and he will lift you up.

The Father is saying, "Set your heart on things above where Christ is seated at the right hand of God." Focus your mind on heavenly things, not on earthly concerns. Your life is now hidden with Christ in God. When Christ appears in your life, you will also appear with Him in glory. I have chosen and appointed you for this time. If you encounter hindering spirits, take authority over them and cast them down in the mighty name of Jesus. Remember, I have given you power over the enemy. Submit to Me, resist the enemy, and he will flee from you in Jesus' name.

JUNE 7th

Breaking Down Barriers

> Ephesians 1:5-7
>
> he predestined us for adoption to sonship through Jesus Christ, in accordance with his pleasure and will— ⁶ to the praise of his glorious grace, which he has freely given us in the One he loves. ⁷ In him we have redemption through his blood, the forgiveness of sins, in accordance with the riches of God's grace

The Father is saying, "Let Me break down the barriers in your life." Some of you have built walls in your relationships for fear of getting hurt. In contrast, others have mental barriers from agreeing with the enemy's lies. Reject these lies and dismantle all deception in the name of Jesus. Remember, the Most High God loves you deeply. You are precious in My sight. You were embraced and accepted when you accepted Christ Jesus as your Lord and Savior. You are My beloved.

JUNE 8ᵀᴴ

Set Apart for a Purpose

Matthew 13:37-39

He answered, "The one who sowed the good seed is the Son of Man. ³⁸ The field is the world, and the good seed stands for the people of the kingdom. The weeds are the people of the evil one, ³⁹ and the enemy who sows them is the devil. The harvest is the end of the age, and the harvesters are angels.

Matthew 10:34

"Do not suppose that I have come to bring peace to the earth. I did not come to bring peace but a sword.

The Father is saying, I am in the process of separating the wheat from the tares. You are set apart for a time such as this, and not everyone can journey with you where I am leading you. While moving away from certain people or situations may be difficult, remember that My grace is sufficient for you. If you find it hard to let go, ask My Holy Spirit for additional grace. You are a chosen generation, and understand that I did not come to bring peace to the earth but a sword. Trust in the process and embrace the purpose I have for you.

JUNE 9TH

God's Faithfulness Through Every Season

Psalm 34:4

I sought the Lord, and he answered me;

he delivered me from all my fears.

The Father is saying, "I am the same God in the valley and on the mountaintop." Even when you walk through the valley of the shadow of death, you need not fear, for I am with you. My rod and staff comfort you." You will overcome no matter your situation, circumstance, or hardship. You are never alone in your struggles. Fight the good fight of faith! I am granting you the grace to persevere and breakthrough. Expect a sudden turnaround in Jesus' name.

JUNE 10ᵀᴴ

Ready to Receive

James 1:7

That person should not expect to receive anything from the Lord.

Malachi 3:6-10

"I, the Lord, do not change. So you, the descendants of Jacob, are not destroyed. ⁷ Ever since the time of your ancestors, you have turned away from my decrees and have not kept them. Return to me, and I will return to you," says the Lord Almighty. "But you ask, 'How are we to return?' ⁸ "Will a mere mortal rob God? Yet you rob me. "But you ask, 'How are we robbing you?' "In tithes and offerings. ⁹ You are under a curse—your whole nation—because you are robbing me. ¹⁰ Bring the whole tithe into the storehouse that there may be food in my house. Test me in this," says the Lord Almighty, "and see if I will not throw open the floodgates of heaven and pour out so much blessing that there will not be room enough to store it.

The Father is saying, "As you journey with me, prepare to receive all that I have planned for you." I have blessings and gifts with your name on them. I am the source of every perfect gift from the Father of Lights, who does not change. Everything I have for you is uniquely yours, unchangeable and secure. I am the LORD and do not change; therefore, you are not consumed. Return to my ordinances, and I will return to you, says the Lord of hosts.

JUNE 11ᵀᴴ

Unchanging Love

Genesis 28:14

Your descendants will be like the dust of the earth, and you will spread out to the west and to the east, to the north and to the south. All peoples on earth will be blessed through you and your offspring.

Numbers 23:19

God is not human, that he should lie, not a human being, that he should change his mind. Does he speak and then not act? Does he promise and not fulfill?

The Father is saying, "Just as the waves constantly move upon the shore, I remain unchanging." My love for you is unconditional and unwavering. My mercy flows continuously to those who are in awe of me. What I have ordained for you is firmly established and cannot be altered. I am not like humans who lie or change their minds. When I speak, I act; when I promise, I fulfill. My plans for you exceed anything you can ask, think, or imagine. Do not fear; I am with you. I will bring your descendants from the east and gather them from the west. I will call to the north and the south, and through you, all the families of the earth will be blessed.

JUNE 12TH

Trust in My Timing

> Matthew 7:7

"Ask, and it will be given to you; seek, and you will find; knock, and the door will be opened to you.

> 1 Samuel 12:17

Is it not wheat harvest now? I will call on the Lord to send thunder and rain. And you will realize what an evil thing you did in the eyes of the Lord when you asked for a king."

The Father is saying, "I understand that you may feel I am distant and that you are experiencing a dry season where progress seems slow. Yet, I am working at my own pace and in my own time." Even if little is happening, know I am moving behind the scenes. Though you face attacks from the enemy, arm yourself with the shield of faith to extinguish all the fiery darts in the name of Jesus. Continue to press forward and trust in me. Trust me with your family, marriage, and children. Do not doubt what I have done for you or what I am about to do. Keep asking, and you will receive; keep seeking and finding; keep knocking, and the door will open.

JUNE 13 ᵀᴴ

Stand Firm in Faith

1 Peter 5:8

Be alert and of sober mind. Your enemy, the devil, prowls around like a roaring lion, looking for someone to devour.

Ephesians 6:10-18

Finally, be strong in the Lord and in his mighty power. ¹¹ Put on the full armor of God so that you can take your stand against the devil's schemes. ¹² For our struggle is not against flesh and blood, but against the rulers, against the authorities, against the powers of this dark world and against the spiritual forces of evil in the heavenly realms. ¹³ Therefore put on the full armor of God, so that when the day of evil comes, you may be able to stand your ground, and after you have done everything, to stand. ¹⁴ Stand firm then, with the belt of truth buckled around your waist, with the breastplate of righteousness in place, ¹⁵ and with your feet fitted with the readiness that comes from the gospel of peace. ¹⁶ In addition to all this, take up the shield of faith, with which you can extinguish all the flaming arrows of the evil one. ¹⁷ Take the helmet of salvation and the sword of the Spirit, which is the word of God. ¹⁸ And pray in the Spirit on all occasions with all kinds of prayers and requests. With this in mind, be alert and always keep on praying for all the Lord's people.

The Father is saying, "Beloved, expect attacks from the adversary and remain vigilant. Your enemy, the devil, roams like a lion, seeking whom he may devour. Equip yourself with the full armor of God to withstand his schemes and tactics." Knowing God's Word personally and remaining steadfast in prayer is crucial. No weapon formed against you will prosper in the mighty name of Jesus. Push through the attacks and trials even when you feel disheartened and struggle to read the Word or praise Me. Remember, you have victory in Christ Jesus!

JUNE 14ᵀᴴ

Pregnant with Purpose

John 16:33

"I have told you these things so that in me you may have peace. In this world, you will have trouble. But take heart! I have overcome the world."

The Father is saying, "You are pregnant with destiny, carrying a divine purpose within you." Your calling will lead you from glory to glory and faith to faith. No enemy or force on earth or in hell can thwart what I have placed inside you. I have called and appointed you, and the increased attacks are a testament to your threat to the kingdom of darkness. Remember, while you will face tribulation, I have overcome it. Victory is assured in My name; nothing can separate you from My love. If I am for you, who can be against you?

JUNE 15ᵀᴴ

Praise Through Every Season

> Ephesians 2:8-9

For it is by grace you have been saved, through faith—and this is not from yourselves, it is the gift of God— ⁹ not by works, so that no one can boast.

> Job 2:10

He replied, "You are talking like a foolish woman. Shall we accept good from God and not trouble?" In all this, Job did not sin in what he said.

The Father is saying to praise and thank Me in all circumstances, whether in times of plenty or seasons of hardship. Just as we receive good from God, we must accept the challenges. Praise Me and express your gratitude through every trial. Even amid storms and difficulties, My grace will see you through. If your faith feels shaken, recall how I have delivered you before. Remember, your salvation comes through faith in Christ Jesus, not by your own efforts. As My beloved child, you are raised with Christ and seated with Him in heavenly places. Do not give up. Keep seeking and knocking; you will receive everything I have prepared for you.

JUNE 16TH

Finding Joy in Trials

James 1:2-4

Consider it pure joy, my brothers and sisters,[a] whenever you face trials of many kinds, ³ because you know that the testing of your faith produces perseverance. ⁴ Let perseverance finish its work so that you may be mature and complete, not lacking anything.

Exodus 14:14

The Lord will fight for you; you need only to be still."

The Father is saying, "Find joy, my beloved, whenever you face trials of many kinds." These challenges test your faith and produce perseverance. Allow perseverance to complete its work so you may become mature and lacking nothing. It is natural to feel confused when events around you don't make sense or lack explanation. Trust in Me fully and follow My will, even when understanding eludes you. Will you step out in faith? Will you move beyond your comfort zone? When faced with false accusations, will you continue to follow Me? Embrace these trials as opportunities to grow and deepen your trust in Me.

JUNE 17TH

The Fight of Faith

Matthew 17:20-22

He replied, "Because you have so little faith. Truly, I tell you, if you have faith as small as a mustard seed, you can say to this mountain, 'Move from here to there,' and it will move. Nothing will be impossible for you." [21]. 22 When they came together in Galilee, he said to them, "The Son of Man is going to be delivered into the hands of men.

James 1:6

But when you ask, you must believe and not doubt because the one who doubts is like a wave of the sea, blown and tossed by the wind.

1 Timothy 6:12

Fight the good fight of the faith. Take hold of the eternal life to which you were called when you made your good confession in the presence of many witnesses.

The Father is saying, "Fight the good fight of faith, even when you can't see or feel the outcome." Trust that everything will unfold according to My plan. I have called you to walk by faith, not by sight. If you were to walk by sight, what kind of faith would that be? Remember, if you have faith the size of a mustard seed, you can move mountains. Every choice to embrace faith over fear strengthens you and increases your resolve. Doubt only makes you unstable, like a wave tossed by the wind. Keep your faith steadfast, and watch how I work in your life.

JUNE 18ᵀᴴ

Unchanging Love in Every Storm

Hebrews 13:8

Jesus Christ is the same yesterday and today and forever.

Romans 11:29

for God's gifts and his call are irrevocable.

The Father is saying that Jesus Christ is the same yesterday, today, and forever. My nature is constant; My love for you never wavers. I am your Abba, and you are My beloved. If your routine has been disrupted, know it is part of My plan. Worship Me through the storm you're facing. Focus on Me, not the waves or the wind. I am with you through every trial. There is peace and joy available in every circumstance. Hold My hand, and together, we will overcome."

JUNE 19ᵀᴴ

Unwavering Presence

John 3:16

For God so loved the world that he gave his one and only Son, that whoever believes in him shall not perish but have eternal life.

Matthew 22:32

'I am the God of Abraham, the God of Isaac, and the God of Jacob'? He is not the God of the dead but of the living."

The Father is saying, "I am who I say I am: the Way, the Truth, and the Life. No one comes to the Father except through Me. I am the God of Abraham, Isaac, and Jacob—the God of the living, not the dead. I am with you through every hardship, storm, battle, and persecution. My presence is constant, my beloved. When taking the next step feels challenging, hold firmly to My hand. I am guiding you, teaching you to rely on My Spirit, and assisting you every step of the way. Continually depend on Me and seek My will above all else."

JUNE 20TH

Guard Against Deception

2 Corinthians 2:11

in order that Satan might not outwit us. For we are not unaware of his schemes.

James 1:2-4

Consider it pure joy, my brothers and sisters, whenever you face trials of many kinds, ³ because you know that the testing of your faith produces perseverance. ⁴ Let perseverance finish its work so that you may be mature and complete, not lacking anything.

The Father is saying that we must not be outwitted by Satan, for we are not ignorant of his schemes. Satan seeks to sow confusion and chaos. He comes only to steal, kill, and destroy, but I have come to give you life and life abundantly. Hold firmly to my promises; what I have promised you is meant for you. Even while testing, be steadfast. The testing of your faith produces perseverance, and perseverance must finish its work so that you may be mature and complete, lacking nothing.

JUNE 21ST

Restoration Through Suffering

Romans 5:1-5

Therefore, since we have been justified through faith, we have peace with God through our Lord Jesus Christ, ² through whom we have gained access by faith into this grace in which we now stand. And we boast in the hope of the glory of God. ³ Not only so, but we also glory in our sufferings because we know that suffering produces perseverance; ⁴ perseverance, character; and character, hope. ⁵ And hope does not put us to shame, because God's love has been poured out into our hearts through the Holy Spirit, who has been given to us

The Father is saying that after you have endured suffering for a little while, the God of all grace, who has called you to His eternal glory in Christ, will restore, confirm, strengthen, and establish you. Suffering is a part of this life, but it will end for those who place their faith in Me alone. I promise restoration from all suffering. Since faith has justified you, you have peace with God through our Lord Jesus Christ. Through Him, we have access by faith to His grace, in which we stand. Rejoice today, knowing that your hope is in Me alone. Remember that suffering produces endurance, endurance produces character, and character produces hope. This hope does not disappoint because God's love has been poured into our hearts through the Holy Spirit and given to us.

JUNE 22ND

Fixing Your Eyes on the Lord

Psalm 121:1-4

I lift up my eyes to the mountains— where does my help come from?² My help comes from the Lord, the Maker of heaven and earth.³ He will not let your foot slip— he who watches over you will not slumber; ⁴ indeed, he who watches over Israel will neither slumber nor sleep.

Isaiah 26:3

You will keep in perfect peace those whose minds are steadfast because they trust in you.

The Father is saying, "Set your heart and mind upon Me. Do not look to the left or right; instead, look up and remember that your help comes from the Lord, the Maker of heaven and earth." I will not let you fall or let your foot be moved; I who keep you will not slumber. Just as I keep Israel, I neither slumber nor sleep. I, the Lord, will keep your mind and soul in perfect peace. When anxiety arises, begin to pray and release every worry to Me. Leave it at My feet and watch how I move on your behalf. You are My beloved, and I keep you in perfect peace because your mind stays on Me, and you trust in Me.

JUNE 23ʳᵈ

Empowered Through Christ

Luke 10:19

I have given you authority to trample on snakes and scorpions and to overcome all the power of the enemy; nothing will harm you.

Matthew 16:19

I will give you the keys of the kingdom of heaven; whatever you bind on earth will be bound in heaven, and whatever you loose on earth will be loosed in heaven."

The Father is saying, "Anything is possible because you can do all things through Christ, who strengthens you!" Though the enemy may try to steal your hope and peace, he cannot succeed. You belong to Me. Take authority over your feelings and emotions, commanding them to align with My will in the name of Jesus. As a child of God, I have given you the power to overcome all the enemy's schemes. Know that I am the King of kings and the Lord of Lords and have granted you access to My kingdom. Whatever you bind on earth will be bound in heaven, and whatever you loose on earth will be loosed in heaven.

JUNE 24ᵀᴴ

Grace for Every Need

Hebrews 4:16

Let us then approach God's throne of grace with confidence so that we may receive mercy and find grace to help us in our time of need.

2 Corinthians 12:8-10

Three times, I pleaded with the Lord to take it away from me. ⁹ But he said to me, "My grace is sufficient for you, for my power is made perfect in weakness." Therefore, I will boast all the more gladly about my weaknesses so that Christ's power may rest on me. ¹⁰ That is why, for Christ's sake, I delight in weaknesses, in insults, in hardships, in persecutions, in difficulties. For when I am weak, then I am strong.

The Father is saying, "Come boldly to My throne of grace to receive mercy and find help in your time of need." Remember to pray for more grace when you struggle in any area of your life. Even though I pleaded three times for relief, I responded, "My grace is sufficient for you, for my power is made perfect in weakness." Therefore, embrace your weaknesses with joy, for my power is most evident in these moments. Rejoice in difficulties, insults, and hardships, knowing that when you are weak, you are strong through My power. My grace is sufficient for every trial and hardship. Ask My Holy Spirit to strengthen you where you need it most, in Jesus' name.

JUNE 25ᵀᴴ

A Crown of Beauty

Psalm 121:1

I lift up my eyes to the mountains— where does my help come from?

John 14:26

But the Advocate, the Holy Spirit, whom the Father will send in my name, will teach you all things and will remind you of everything I have said to you.

The Father is saying to those who mourn: I will give you a crown of beauty instead of ashes, a joyous blessing in place of mourning, and festive praise instead of despair. I am your God and will comfort you in times of trouble and rescue you when needed. Look to the hills; your help comes from the LORD, the Maker of heaven and earth. In everything aligned with My will, I will stretch out My hand to help you because I am your Father and love you deeply. Do not doubt what I can do through and in you—only trust Me. I watch over you tirelessly; neither slumber nor sleep will touch My care for you. The sun will not harm you by day, nor the moon by night. My Spirit will guide you into all truth, and the truth will set you free. You are never alone; the Holy Spirit is your Advocate, helping and empowering you in every way.

JUNE 26ᵀᴴ

Restoration and Renewal

Joel 2:25

"I will repay you for the years the locusts have eaten— the great locust and the young locust, the other locusts and the locust swarm—my great army that I sent among you.

Leviticus 20:7

"'Consecrate yourselves and be holy, because I am the Lord your God.

The Father is saying, "I will repay you for the years the locusts have eaten—the great locusts, the young locusts, and the locust swarms. I will restore everything that the enemy has stolen from you." Rejoice and remember that I am a loving, merciful God. You are mine, and I have rescued you from bondage by My mighty right hand. This restoration will come not by might nor power but by the Spirit of the living God. I am holy, and I promise to restore and bless you. Even if you have brought trouble upon yourself through your actions, I will still provide and renew what has been lost. I have chosen you for this time, my beloved. Thank Me for everything I am doing and for what I will do. Give Me all the praise and worship, for I am God alone.

JUNE 27TH

Hope in the Midst of Trials

Psalm 34:17-20

The righteous cry out, and the Lord hears them; he delivers them from all their troubles. [18] The Lord is close to the brokenhearted and saves those who are crushed in spirit. [19] The righteous person may have many troubles, but the Lord delivers him from them all; [20] he protects all his bones, not one of them will be broken.

Jeremiah 29:14

I will be found by you," declares the Lord, "and will bring you back from captivity. I will gather you from all the nations and places where I have banished you," declares the Lord, "and will bring you back to the place from which I carried you into exile."

The Father is saying: "I give hope to the hopeless. Do not fear, my beloved, for I am with you. When the righteous cry for help, I deliver them from all their troubles. I am near the brokenhearted and save those crushed in spirit. Though many are the afflictions of the righteous, I deliver them from all. I protect every part of you; none of your bones are broken. If you are facing seemingly hopeless situations, remember that I am bringing you out of captivity. I will restore your fortunes, gather you from all nations and places where I have scattered you, and bring you back to where you were exiled.

JUNE 28TH

Seated with Christ: Embracing Your Divine Position

Romans 12:2

Do not conform to the pattern of this world, but be transformed by the renewing of your mind. Then, you will be able to test and approve what God's will is—his good, pleasing, and perfect will.

Psalm 100:4

Enter his gates with thanksgiving and his courts with praise; give thanks to him and praise his name.

The Father says, I have raised you with Christ and seated you with Him in His heavenly kingdom. You are now My people, chosen and appointed for such a time. Whatever discouragement you face today, release it to Me and lay it all at My feet. I am listening to everything you say. Pour out your heart to Me—I want to comfort, strengthen, and encourage you. As you enter My gates with thanksgiving and My courts with praise, fill every part of yourself with My presence. Remember, bringing thankfulness and praise to My holy name is an act of worship. When negative emotions arise, renew your mind with My Word and be transformed. You will discern My will through this renewal—what is good, acceptable, and perfect.

JUNE 29TH

Guarding Your Words: Embracing the Call to Holiness

1 Peter 3:10

For "Whoever would love life and see good days must keep their tongue from evil and their lips from deceitful speech.

Revelation 21:8

But the cowardly, the unbelieving, the vile, the murderers, the sexually immoral, those who practice magic arts, the idolaters, and all liars—they will be consigned to the fiery lake of burning sulfur. This is the second death."

The Father is saying if you desire to love life and see good days, guard your tongue from evil and avoid engaging in harmful speech. Speaking evil about others is a serious matter akin to witchcraft. If you gossip or speak negatively about others, repent from these actions. Remember, those who practice evil, including witchcraft, idolatry, and dishonesty, face severe consequences. Repent and turn away from such behaviors, for the kingdom of God is near. Embrace holiness and let your words reflect the love and purity I desire for you.

JUNE 30ᵀᴴ

Complete Healing at the Altar

Acts 3:6

Then Peter said, "Silver or gold I do not have, but what I do have I give you. In the name of Jesus Christ of Nazareth, walk."

Psalm 95:6

Come, let us bow down in worship; let us kneel before the Lord, our Maker;

The Father is saying, "Come to the altar and allow me to cleanse you from all iniquities." I desire to make you whole, and only by my hand can you find true completeness. Open your heart to me, and I will fill every part of your life with my presence. Be transparent about your struggles, even those you find hard to discuss. I am your Father, and you are my beloved. If you need healing, touch the affected area of your body and command it to be healed in the mighty name of Jesus. As Peter said, "Silver or gold I do not have, but what I do have, I give you: in the name of Jesus Christ of Nazareth, walk." Trust in my power to restore and heal.

JULY 1ST

The Best Is Yet to Come

Isaiah 43:19

See, I am doing a new thing! Now it springs up; do you not perceive it? I am making a way in the wilderness and streams in the wasteland.

The Father is saying that He has reserved the best for last. He teaches you how to wage spiritual warfare and fight against the enemy. There have been moments when you felt like giving up, but you persevered, and that's why the best is yet to come. The Father has a grand surprise in store for you. Because you didn't give in, He will not relent; He is about to amaze you. As you emerge from your trials, He prepares to bring you through the desert and guide you to a new job promotion. Today marks the beginning of a new month, a new day. Pay close attention: the Father is doing something new. It is already springing forth—can you not see it? He will make a way in the wilderness and provide rivers in the desert.

JULY 2ND

Trust in the Unknown

John 13:7

Jesus replied, "You do not realize now what I am doing, but later you will understand."

James 1:7

That person should not expect to receive anything from the Lord.

The Father is saying that even when you face challenges beyond your understanding, it is not your role to comprehend everything but to trust Him in all you do. Today, express your gratitude for every trial and every experience by thanking Him for the freedom of His presence in your life. Remember Jesus' words: "What I am doing, you do not understand now, but you will know after this." His grace is sufficient for every aspect of your life. Ask the Holy Spirit to increase grace where you need it most, allowing His presence to overflow. The Most High God loves you deeply.

JULY 3RD

Stay Focused on Your Calling

Exodus 14:19-31

Then, the angel of God, who had been traveling in front of Israel's army, withdrew and went behind them. The pillar of cloud also moved from in front and stood behind them, ²⁰ coming between the armies of Egypt and Israel. Throughout the night, the cloud brought darkness to the one side and light to the other side, so neither went near the other all night long. ²¹ Then Moses stretched out his hand over the sea, and all that night, the Lord drove the sea back with a strong east wind and turned it into dry land. The waters were divided, ²², and the Israelites went through the sea on dry ground, with a wall of water on their right and on their left. ²³ The Egyptians pursued them, and all Pharaoh's horses and chariots and horsemen followed them into the sea. ²⁴ During the last watch of the night, the Lord looked down from the pillar of fire and cloud at the Egyptian army and threw it into confusion.²⁵ He jammed the wheels of their chariots so that they had difficulty driving. And the Egyptians said, "Let's get away from the Israelites! The Lord is fighting for them against Egypt." ²⁶ Then the Lord said to Moses, "Stretch out your hand over the sea so that the waters may flow back over the Egyptians and their chariots and horsemen." ²⁷ Moses stretched out his hand over the sea, and at daybreak, the sea went back to its place. The Egyptians were fleeing toward it, and the Lord swept them into the sea. ²⁸ The water flowed back and covered the chariots and horsemen—the entire army of Pharaoh that had followed the Israelites into the sea. Not one of them survived. ²⁹ But the Israelites went through the sea on dry ground, with a wall of water on their right and on their left. ³⁰ That day, the Lord saved Israel from the hands of the Egyptians, and Israel saw the Egyptians lying dead on the shore. ³¹ And when the Israelites saw the mighty hand of the Lord displayed against the Egyptians, the people feared the Lord and put their trust in him and in Moses, his servant.

Isaiah 43:2

When you pass through the waters, I will be with you;

and when you pass through the rivers, they will not sweep over you. When you walk through the fire, you will not be burned; the flames will not set you ablaze.

The Father is saying that you should resist the enemy's distractions that divert you from your divine purpose. The enemy employs various tactics—through people, situations, and devices—to keep you from fulfilling your calling. Be vigilant against these schemes and bind every demonic force in the powerful name of Jesus. Do not let the evil one steal your peace. Decide today to stand firm against all demonic tactics by immersing yourself in the Word of God, staying consecrated to Him, and depending on His presence daily. Trust and obey His commandments, and keep your focus on Him. He leads you to deeper places where your enemies cannot follow, parting the Red Sea for you as He did for Moses. He promises you a peace that only He can provide—a supernatural peace that surpasses all understanding.

JULY 4ᵀᴴ

Celebrate Every Victory

1 Corinthians 10:13

No temptation has overtaken you except what is common to mankind. And God is faithful; he will not let you be tempted beyond what you can bear. But when you are tempted, he will also provide a way out so that you can endure it.

John 16:33

"I have told you these things so that in me you may have peace. In this world, you will have trouble. But take heart! I have overcome the world."

The Father is saying that you should celebrate every victory you achieve together. Each triumph is a testament to our shared strength. Every time you pass a test, it is a victory. When you fall but rise again, it is a victory. Each time you resist temptation or choose prayer over frustration, it is a victory. In every aspect of your life—relationships, service, or ministry—acknowledge that we have overcome challenges together. I am your help, beloved, and together we can face anything, one day and one task at a time, in Jesus' name. Trust in God's faithfulness; He will not let you be tempted beyond your capacity. There is no need to worry, for you are held securely in the palm of His hand. You are deeply loved!

JULY 5TH

Secure in Christ

Ephesians 1:13

And you also were included in Christ when you heard the message of truth, the gospel of your salvation. When you believed, you were marked in him with a seal, the promised Holy Spirit,

Isaiah 54:17

no weapon forged against you will prevail, and you will refute every tongue that accuses you. This is the heritage of the servants of the Lord, and this is their vindication from me," declares the Lord.

The Father is saying that you were included in Christ when you heard the message of truth—the gospel of your salvation. By believing, you were marked with a seal, the promised Holy Spirit, who serves as a deposit guaranteeing your inheritance until the redemption of God's people, to the praise of His glory. This seal means you are protected from the enemy. Though he may attack, he cannot touch or overpower you. God is with you and within you. No demon or force can harm you. The enemy may try to intimidate you, but his efforts are in vain. Remember, no weapon formed against you will succeed. Take heart, beloved, for Jesus has overcome the world.

JULY 6ᵀᴴ

A Foundation of Unshakable Strength

Deuteronomy 26:9

He brought us to this place and gave us this land, a land flowing with milk and honey;

Isaiah 33:6

He will be the sure foundation for your times, a rich store of salvation and wisdom and knowledge; the fear of the Lord is the key to this treasure.

The Father is saying that the enemy is bewildered; he cannot understand why you continue to praise and worship. The Lord your God is speaking. That last attack was meant to bring you down, but I protected you. My hand is upon you; the enemy cannot even find you. I am with you—within, beside, behind, and all around you. I am your Lord and your God; you will not be shaken or moved, for the foundation you stand on is solid rock. The Lord is honored, residing in heaven. I will fill Zion's people with justice and righteousness. I will be the firm foundation for your entire life. I will lead you, my beloved, guiding you in all truth. You will not be distracted. I will show you the path to take. I have brought you to a place, granting you this land flowing with milk and honey.

JULY 7ᵀᴴ

Trusting in Divine Guidance

Hebrews 12:2

fixing our eyes on Jesus, the pioneer and perfecter of faith. For the joy set before him, he endured the cross, scorning its shame, and sat down at the right hand of the throne of God.

Habakkuk 2:2-3

Then the Lord replied: "Write down the revelation and make it plain on tablets so that a herald may run with it. ³ For the revelation awaits an appointed time; it speaks of the end and will not prove false. Though it linger, wait for it; it will certainly come and will not delay.

The Father is saying, "I am not the God of confusion. Confusion comes from the enemy, who has been deceiving since Adam and Eve. I am in control." Will you relinquish control so I can guide you how I desire for you? My path is better; my ways are greater for you. Look to Jesus, the author and finisher of your faith, who endured the cross with joy set before Him, despising the shame, and now sits at the right hand of the throne of God. I am your helper and friend, always listening and ready to provide all you need—whether provision or vision. I am your Lord God, prepared to supply all your needs. I am yours, and you are mine.

JULY 8TH

Embracing New Creation

2 Corinthians 5:14-21

For Christ's love compels us because we are convinced that one died for all, and therefore all died. ¹⁵ And he died for all that those who live should no longer live for themselves but for him who died for them and was raised again. ¹⁶ So, from now on, we regard no one from a worldly point of view. Though we once regarded Christ in this way, we do so no longer.¹⁷ Therefore, if anyone is in Christ, the new creation has come:[a]The old has gone, the new is here! ¹⁸ All this is from God, who reconciled us to himself through Christ and gave us the ministry of reconciliation: ¹⁹ that God was reconciling the world to himself in Christ, not counting people's sins against them. And he has committed to us the message of reconciliation. ²⁰ We are, therefore, Christ's ambassadors, as though God were making his appeal through us. We implore you on Christ's behalf: Be reconciled to God. ²¹ God made him who had no sin to be sin[b]for us so that in him we might become the righteousness of God.

Revelation 20:10

And the devil, who deceived them, was thrown into the lake of burning sulfur, where the beast and the false prophet had been thrown. They will be tormented day and night forever and ever.

The Father is saying, "Allow my presence to renew every part of your being. As I restore you to order, every fear you have will be dismantled." I am the God who restores all. When you surrendered your life to me, everything from before Christ died, you are now a new creation in Christ

Jesus. Therefore, if anyone is in Christ, he is a new creation; old things have passed away, and all things have become new. When the enemy reminds you of your past, remind him of his future. The devil, who deceived them, will be cast into the lake of burning sulfur, where the beast and the false prophet have been thrown. This is the devil's future—eternal torment in the lake of fire. Rebuke and take authority over every lie and cast it back to the abyss in the name of Jesus.

JULY 9TH

Deep Calls to Deep

> Jeremiah 29:11

For I know the plans I have for you," declares the Lord, "plans to prosper you and not to harm you, plans to give you hope and a future.

The Father is saying, "Deep calls to deep. Even when your waves and breakers have swept over you, and you feel overwhelmed by the roar of your struggles, call out to my name." My presence desires to fill you, from the crown of your head to the soles of your feet. My presence is my Holy Spirit dwelling within you. I want to be where you are, my beloved. You have never gone too far for my arm to reach you. I am with you every step of the way. For I know my plans for you declares the Lord—plans to prosper you and not to harm you, plans to give you hope and a future.

JULY 10TH

Comfort in the Darkest Valley

> Psalm 23:4

Even though I walk through the darkest valley, I will fear no evil, for you are with me; your rod and your staff, they comfort me.

> Psalm 23:3

he refreshes my soul. He guides me along the right paths for his name's sake.

The Father says, "Even though you walk through the darkest valley, you will fear no evil. I am with you; my rod and staff will comfort you." Despite your trials, I am present in the valley, supplying you with every need, and I am ready to pour out my living water upon you. You may encounter hardships, but I am guiding you, speaking to you, and leading you in the right direction. Though you may feel weak, my Spirit is strong within you. Remember who walks with you, guides you, and communicates with you daily. I will never leave you nor forsake you, my beloved. You are forever mine. I am the one who restores your soul.

JULY 11TH

Embracing the Weight of Glory

Revelation 1:1

The revelation from Jesus Christ, which God gave him to show his servants what must soon take place. He made it known by sending his angel to his servant John,

2 Peter 3:18

But grow in the grace and knowledge of our Lord and Savior Jesus Christ. To him be glory both now and forever! Amen.

The Father is saying, "The anointing I have placed on your life comes with pressure and attacks." The mantle you carry holds significant weight in the spirit realm. You have entered a new dimension and a higher level. The spiritual warfare was intense, but you did not face it alone; I, the Lord your God, pushed you through. You now carry a weight of glory wherever you go, which is why people notice. You are different, beloved, not because of who you are but because of the mantle I have placed on you. It is the glory of Jesus in your life. Rejoice, for you have made it through the trials by my grace. You persevered through the attacks and the warfare. Praise my holy name for your journey into new dimensions. You have overcome challenges that others could not, and you emerged victorious beloved.

JULY 12TH

Embracing New Beginnings

2 Corinthians 5:17

Therefore, if anyone is in Christ, the new creation has come: The old has gone, the new is here!

Ephesians 3:20

Now to him who is able to do immeasurably more than all we ask or imagine, according to his power that is at work within us,

The Father is saying, "I am stirring up something new in your life: new relationships, new beginnings, and a new version of yourself." I have removed all things and people that are not from me. You have prayed to remove anything or anyone I did not send, and that is exactly what I have done. I am placing new things and people into your life. Therefore, anyone in Christ is a new creation; old things have passed away, and all things have become new. Glory to God! Your old life is gone; it is dead. Behold, I am giving you a new life in Christ Jesus. It is time to release the past and move forward into the bright future I have prepared for you. Oh, my beloved, I have so much in store for you.

JULY 13TH

Embracing Divine Renewal

Isaiah 61:3

and provide for those who grieve in Zion— to bestow on them a crown of beauty instead of ashes, the oil of joy instead of mourning, and a garment of praise instead of a spirit of despair. They will be called oaks of righteousness, a planting of the Lord for the display of his splendor.

Matthew 11:28-30

Come to me, all you who are weary and burdened, and I will give you rest. ²⁹ Take my yoke upon you and learn from me, for I am gentle and humble in heart, and you will find rest for your souls. ³⁰ For my yoke is easy, and my burden is light."

The Father is saying, "I am continually moving in your life, downloading new strategies and ideas into your spirit for the next assignment." Allow me to remove anything that doesn't belong in your life. As I remove these false burdens, I will replace them with praise and thanksgiving. I will appoint those who mourn in Zion a crown of beauty instead of ashes, festive oil instead of mourning, and splendid clothes instead of despair. They will be called righteous trees, planted by the Lord to glorify Him.

JULY 14TH

Unshakable Protection

Psalm 139:14

I praise you because I am fearfully and wonderfully made; your works are wonderful; I know that full well.

Isaiah 41:13

For I am the Lord your God who takes hold of your right hand and says to you, Do not fear; I will help you.

The Father is saying, "No weapon formed against you shall prosper." The attacks against your marriage, your children, and your finances will not succeed in Jesus' name. You may feel the pressure of these attacks, but remember, the devil can do nothing without permission. Focus your attention on me, set your heart on me, and do not look to the left or the right. Keep your head held high, knowing who you are. You are my child, precious in my sight, fearfully and wonderfully made. When doubt or confusion arises, take authority over it and cast it back into the abyss in the name of Jesus. You are a child of the Most High God.

JULY 15TH

Strength Through Christ

Mark 9:23

'If you can't?" said Jesus. "Everything is possible for one who believes."

Ephesians 2:14-17

For he himself is our peace, who has made the two groups one and has destroyed the barrier, the dividing wall of hostility, ¹⁵ by setting aside in his flesh the law with its commands and regulations. His purpose was to create in himself one new humanity out of the two, thus making peace, ¹⁶ and in one body to reconcile both of them to God through the cross, by which he put to death their hostility. ¹⁷ He came and preached peace to you who were far away and peace to those who were near.

The Father is saying, "You can do all things through Christ who gives you strength—not just some things, but all things." Seek my face and inquire about your assignments to understand what I have graced you for. It is crucial to know your divine calling. Come to me in the secret place, my beloved. Your strength alone is insufficient, but you can achieve far more with my strength. When you feel depleted and unable to continue, ask my Holy Spirit to help you overcome every barrier, task, and assignment in Jesus' name. Together, we will accomplish everything. When you feel drained, ask yourself if you rely on your strength or mine. Allow me to guide you through each day and moment. We can do this together."

JULY 16TH

Trusting in My Perfect Will

> Luke 12:24

Consider the ravens: They do not sow or reap; they have no storeroom or barn, yet God feeds them. And how much more valuable you are than birds!

> Psalm 46:10

He says, "Be still, and know that I am God; I will be exalted among the nations; I will be exalted in the earth."

The Father is saying, "Do not doubt my perfect will for your life. When you doubt, it saddens my heart." I am your Father and know what is best for you, my beloved. The anxiety you experience is often due to a lack of trust. You worry too much about the future and the unknown. Trust me in every area of your life—your marriage, your children, and your finances. Let us face each day together, knowing we can get through anything. Remember the ravens: they do not sow or reap; they have no storeroom or barn, yet I provide for them. How much more valuable are you than the birds?"

JULY 17TH

Perfect Peace Through Trust

John 14:27

Peace I leave with you; my peace I give you. I do not give to you as the world gives. Do not let your hearts be troubled, and do not be afraid.

The Father is saying, "I will keep you in perfect peace when your mind has stayed on me because you trust in me. Maintain a heart posture that remains aligned with me. Invite my Holy Spirit to search your heart and cleanse it from all unrighteousness. I desire to purify your heart and elevate you to new heights and experiences. Allow my Spirit to move and restore order in your life. I leave you with my peace, surpassing what the world offers. Let not your hearts be troubled or afraid."

JULY 18ᵀᴴ

Embracing My Presence

Isaiah 44:2

This is what the Lord says— he who made you, who formed you in the womb, and who will help you: Do not be afraid, Jacob, my servant, Jeshurun, whom I have chosen.

The Father is saying, "As this day unfolds, be mindful of my precious presence." Praise my holy name, and let my presence fill every part of your being. My creations are my birds singing, the beautiful skies, and the clouds. I am your Creator; you were under my care before birth. Do not be terrified, Israel. I understand the many thoughts racing through your mind about the future. Invite my Holy Spirit to captivate every thought and make it obedient to Christ. Let my Spirit guide you in all truth. As the heavens are higher than the earth, so are my ways."

JULY 19TH

Embracing Divine Peace

Ephesians 1:7

In Him, we have redemption through his blood, the forgiveness of sins, in accordance with the riches of God's grace.

2 Timothy 1:7

For the Spirit God gave us does not make us timid but gives us power, love, and self-discipline.

The Father is saying, "I give you peace, but not as the world gives." It is a supernatural peace that only I can provide. I want my children to experience this peace in every area. If you lack peace, ask my Holy Spirit to reveal what you have not fully surrendered. What burdens are you holding onto instead of laying them at my feet? Many of my children lay their burdens down only to pick them up again, dwelling on the same worries and fears. Fear and worry are not your portion; I am your portion. I am your peace, the great I AM. Ask my Holy Spirit to extend grace to help you lay down these issues and never take them back in Jesus' name."

JULY 20th

Flowing with Divine Words

Isaiah 26:3

You will keep in perfect peace those whose minds are steadfast because they trust in you.

Acts 1:2

Until the day he was taken up to heaven after giving instructions through the Holy Spirit to the apostles he had chosen.

The Father is saying, "Rivers of living water will flow from your innermost being." I will place tongues of fire upon your mouth and baptize you with new tongues. When you speak, I will provide the words you need. Do not worry about how to address the assignment I have given you; my words will flow from you like a river. By faith in me alone, speak what I instruct you. I am filling you from the crown of your head to the soles of your feet. Just as on the day of Pentecost, when they were all in one place with one accord, there came a sound from heaven like a rushing mighty wind, filling the house where they were sitting, so will I fill you with my presence and power.

JULY 21ST

Finding Peace Amidst Warfare

> Psalm 55:22

Cast your cares on the Lord, and he will sustain you; he will never let the righteous be shaken.

> Galatians 6:2

Carry each other's burdens, and in this way, you will fulfill the law of Christ.

The Father is saying, "The warfare you face is for the glory of Jesus Christ, the one true King. I am capable of doing more than you can ask or imagine." Lay down every burden you've been carrying, the heavy weight on your shoulders—whether it concerns family, friends, or finances. Release all of this to me today. I desire for all my children to experience perfect peace. I will grant you peace in both your heart and mind. Allow me to saturate and cover you with my peace, my beloved.

JULY 22ND

Peace in the Midst of Warfare

> Deuteronomy 28:8

The Lord will send a blessing on your barns and on everything you put your hand to. The Lord your God will bless you in the land he is giving you.

> 1 Chronicles 16:11

Look to the Lord and his strength; seek his face always.

The Father is saying, "The warfare you are enduring serves to glorify Jesus Christ, the one true King. I can do far more than you can ask or imagine." Lay down every burden you have been carrying—the weight that feels heavy on your shoulders, including worries about family, friends, and finances. Release all of this to me today. I desire for all my children to experience perfect peace. I will provide peace for your heart and mind. Allow me to envelop you with my peace, my beloved."

JULY 23ʳᵈ

Overcoming Temptation with Divine Strength

1 Corinthians 10:13

No temptation has overtaken you except what is common to mankind. And God is faithful; he will not let you be tempted beyond what you can bear. But when you are tempted, he will also provide a way out so that you can endure it.

Isaiah 55:11

so is my word that goes out from my mouth: It will not return to me empty but will accomplish what I desire and achieve the purpose for which I sent it.

The Father is saying, "Do not give up. I know the attacks you are facing, but remember the God you serve." I am greater than any temptation or lie. Circumstances do not make the enemy more powerful than me. I am a great God—bigger than life's challenges and any attack or trial you face today in Jesus' name. Do not believe the enemy's lies; trust every word I have spoken over your life. What I have declared will come to pass. Take every thought captive and make it obedient to Christ Jesus. No temptation you face is beyond human experience or resistance, for I am faithful to my word. I am compassionate and trustworthy, and I will not let you be tempted beyond your ability to endure. With every temptation, I will also provide a way out so you can overcome them joyfully.

JULY 24ᵀᴴ

Embracing Divine Plans

Colossians 3:2-10

Set your minds on things above, not on earthly things. ³ For you died, and your life is now hidden with Christ in God. ⁴ When Christ, who is your[a] life, appears, then you also will appear with him in glory.⁵ Put to death, therefore, whatever belongs to your earthly nature: sexual immorality, impurity, lust, evil desires, and greed, which is idolatry. ⁶ Because of these, the wrath of God is coming.[b] ⁷ You used to walk in these ways, in the life you once lived.⁸ But now you must also rid yourselves of all such things as these: anger, rage, malice, slander, and filthy language from your lips. ⁹ Do not lie to each other, since you have taken off your old self with its practices ¹⁰ and have put on the new self, which is being renewed in knowledge in the image of its Creator.

The Father is saying, "Do not be discouraged when things don't go as planned. I have different plans for you today. Continue to seek me with your whole heart, and you will find me, I promise. Do not look to people for what only I can provide. People will fail and let you down, as they, too, need a Savior—me. My love is the only love that never fails or disappoints. Focus your mind on things above, not on earthly matters. For you have died to your old self, and your life is now hidden with Christ in God. Ask my Holy Spirit to cleanse your heart from all unrighteousness. I want to do something new in your life."

JULY 25ᵀᴴ

Starting the Day with Praise

Jeremiah 29:11

For I know the plans I have for you," declares the Lord, "plans to prosper you and not to harm you, plans to give you hope and a future.

The Father is saying, "Begin this day with praise and thanksgiving." My presence is an open door, responding to your gratitude. Continually thank me for everything I am doing and what I will do in your life. I understand that some days are more challenging than others, but do not give up or believe the enemy's lies. Align your thoughts with my Word and my promises, for my Word is truth. As you delve deeper into the Scriptures, the lies will dissipate, and my voice will become clearer than the whispers of the enemy. Whenever you struggle to believe the truth, ask my Holy Spirit to captivate your mind and bring peace to your soul in the name of Jesus."

JULY 26TH

Guiding Emotions with the Holy Spirit

Jeremiah 29:11

For I know the plans I have for you," declares the Lord, "plans to prosper you and not to harm you, plans to give you hope and a future.

Isaiah 42:16

I will lead the blind by ways they have not known; along unfamiliar paths, I will guide them; I will turn the darkness into light before them and make the rough places smooth. These are the things I will do; I will not forsake them.

The Father is saying, "When your emotions are unsettled, and you feel swayed by different feelings, ask my Holy Spirit to lead you." Let the Spirit take control of your emotions and submit them to me. Never allow temporary emotions to guide your decisions; always follow the Holy Spirit. Allow the Spirit to direct you throughout this day. I desire to provide you with everything you need today, filling you with hope and peace. Trust in me with all your heart, soul, and mind. I will lead you on journeys you've never experienced and to places you've never seen. I am God alone."

JULY 27TH

Conquering Every Enemy

> Matthew 27:32

As they were going out, they met a man from Cyrene, named Simon, and they forced him to carry the cross.

> Matthew 28:5

The angel said to the women, "Do not be afraid, for I know that you are looking for Jesus, who was crucified.

The Father is saying, "It is time to overcome every enemy in your life, whether it be fear, anxiety, doubt, or defeat." It pains me to see my children struggling with these things when, at the cross, it was finished. I bore the nails and endured mockery so you, my beloved, would not suffer. This is true love—saving you from suffering and from hell itself. I lifted you from the pit and set your feet on a solid foundation. Remember all I have done for you and trust that every word I have spoken will come to pass in Jesus' name."

JULY 28TH

Overcoming Distractions

Proverbs 4:25

Let your eyes look straight ahead; fix your gaze directly before you.

Romans 8:14-17

For those who are led by the Spirit of God are the children of God. ¹⁵ The Spirit you received does not make you slaves so that you live in fear again; rather, the Spirit you received brought about your adoption to sonship.[a] And by him we cry, *"Abba,* Father." ¹⁶ The Spirit himself testifies with our spirit that we are God's children. ¹⁷ Now if we are children, then we are heirs—heirs of God and co-heirs with Christ, if indeed we share in his sufferings in order that we may also share in his glory.

The Father is saying, "Do not focus on the enemy's plots, plans, or schemes." One of his primary tactics is distraction, using people, places, and things to divert your attention. Take authority over every unlawful spirit and command it to be cast back into the abyss in Jesus' name. I have created you to live in perfect peace and harmony. Keep your eyes fixed straight ahead and ignore the distractions on the periphery. I am in control and hold the whole world in my hands. When distractions and attacks come your way, do not be intimidated. I will guide you throughout this day, leading you forward."

JULY 29ᵀᴴ

Embracing Divine Timing

1 Corinthians 14:33

For God is not a God of disorder but of peace—as in all the congregations of the Lord's people.

John 14:3

And if I go and prepare a place for you, I will come back and take you to be with me so that you also may be where I am.

The Father says, "I am constantly working and moving on your behalf. What once didn't work will now come to fruition in Jesus' name, and what used to work may no longer be effective". It simply wasn't the right time for that job or the answer to your prayer. Go ahead and try again; you will see success now. I am a God of order and peace, not of disorder. I am always protecting my beloveds. You wouldn't have been ready if I had given you what you asked for earlier. As I prepare you, you are growing and bearing much fruit in Jesus' name.

JULY 30TH

Embracing the Process

Romans 5:4-6

Perseverance, character, and character hope. ⁵ And hope does not put us to shame, because God's love has been poured out into our hearts through the Holy Spirit, who has been given to us. ⁶ You see, at just the right time, when we were still powerless, Christ died for the ungodly.

John 15:2

He cuts off every branch in me that bears no fruit, while every branch that does bear fruit he prunes so that it will be even more fruitful.

The Father is saying, "Do not underestimate the importance of the process you are going through." It is essential for your growth and development. I am strengthening you and working on your character. Many of my children want to rush this process, but it unfolds in time. I am continually moving on your behalf, removing what no longer serves you and replacing it with what is good. I want all my children to bear fruit in Jesus' name. Rejoice amid problems and trials, for they develop endurance, which builds character and strengthens your confident hope of salvation.

JULY 31ST

Proud of Your Faithfulness

Exodus 14:14

The Lord will fight for you; you need only to be still."

Deuteronomy 1:30

The Lord your God, who is going before you, will fight for you, as he did for you in Egypt, before your very eyes,

The Father is saying, "I am so proud of you, my beloved. I know it can be difficult to rise each morning because of the attacks you face." The enemy may throw depression and troubling thoughts your way, but remember, these are external assaults. I see the days when pushing forward and pressing into me is hard. Know that I am with you every step of the way. Even when your flesh feels weary and needs encouragement, you still get up, dress, and serve others. Your choice to put others' needs before your own reflects your discipleship. I see you, and I am so proud of you."

AUGUST 1ST

Embracing New Beginnings

Isaiah 43:19

See, I am doing a new thing! Now it springs up; do you not perceive it? I am making a way in the wilderness and streams in the wasteland.

1 Kings 18:43-46

"Go and look toward the sea," he told his servant. And he went up and looked. "There is nothing there," he said. Seven times, Elijah said, "Go back." 44 The seventh time, the servant reported, "A cloud as small as a man's hand is rising from the sea." So Elijah said, "Go and tell Ahab, 'Hitch up your chariot and go down before the rain stops you.'" 45 Meanwhile, the sky grew black with clouds, the wind rose, a heavy rain started falling, and Ahab rode off to Jezreel. 46 The power of the Lord came on Elijah, and, tucking his cloak into his belt, he ran ahead of Ahab all the way to Jezreel.

The Father is saying, "This month marks a time of new opportunities and fresh starts—out with the old and in with the new." I am pouring living water over the dry areas of your life. The old situations that have caused pain and suffering will no longer affect you. Today, I am removing them and replacing them with joy and more joy. Everything is being made new in Jesus' name. Behold, I am doing a new thing; now it springs forth. Do you not perceive it? I am opening doors that no one can shut and offering new opportunities only I can provide. I will make a way in the wilderness and rivers in the desert for you, my beloved. Revisit the areas where you have seen no movement or increase; check again. The doors that will open will do so with ease, not difficulty. I am removing the enemy's hold, and nothing will be kept from you. Check again.

AUGUST 2ND

Anointed for Spiritual Warfare

Romans 8:6-7

⁶ The mind governed by the flesh is death, but the mind governed by the Spirit is life and peace. ⁷ The mind governed by the flesh is hostile to God; it does not submit to God's law, nor can it do so.

2 Corinthians 10:4

The weapons we fight with are not the weapons of the world. On the contrary, they have divine power to demolish strongholds.

The Father is saying, "I have anointed you to dismantle the kingdom of hell." This anointing comes with challenges and attacks, but I have equipped you for them. Do not be discouraged by the enemy's attempts to unsettle you; remember, he is already defeated and under your feet. Warfare is part of the journey, but I am with you. You did not choose me; I chose you.

The weight of the anointing is significant. Your hands are anointed for spiritual battles, not physical ones. This is spiritual warfare—a battle for the souls in my kingdom. I am deeply saddened to see my people trapped by the enemy's lies and remaining in bondage. The devil has been deceiving since the beginning, but I desire my people to be free, believing in the truth that sets them free.

If you feel heaviness in your hands, it is the anointing that breaks the yoke of bondage. I am setting my people free, and you have embraced this assignment with obedience and trust. Not everyone will understand, but remember that I have anointed you for this time. The weapons of our warfare are not carnal but mighty through God to pull down strongholds. Continue in faith and trust in me alone.

AUGUST 3ʳᵈ

Beyond Time and Space

2 Chronicles 2:6

The punishment inflicted on him by the majority is sufficient.

Genesis 2:7

Then the Lord God formed a man[a] from the dust of the ground and breathed into his nostrils the breath of life, and the man became a living being.

The Father is saying, "I am not confined by time or space." Do you not know? Have you not heard? Has it not been revealed since the foundation of the earth? I sit enthroned above the circle of the world, and its people are like grasshoppers to me. I stretch out the heavens like a canopy and spread them out like a tent to dwell in. I am omnipresent, present everywhere at once. There is nothing I cannot see or hear. I am not limited by space. I created the heavens and the earth, and everything exists by my breath. I formed humanity from the dust and breathed the breath of life into their nostrils. Remember that I am always with you beyond the limits of time and space.

AUGUST 4ᵀᴴ

Trusting Through Trials

James 1:2-3

Consider it pure joy, my brothers and sisters, whenever you face trials of many kinds, ³ because you know that the testing of your faith produces perseverance.

1 Peter 1:6-7

In all this, you greatly rejoice, though now, for a little while, you may have had to suffer grief in all kinds of trials. ⁷ These have come so that the proven genuineness of your faith—of greater worth than gold, which perishes even though refined by fire—may result in praise, glory, and honor when Jesus Christ is revealed.

The Father is saying, "You will get through these times of testing and trials." You will overcome. I will hold you up with my righteous right hand and never let you go. Even amid challenges, I will support you. Remember, you are not alone. Focus on one day at a time; do not dwell on the future, as it often brings doubt and fear. Instead of complaining and overthinking, release your concerns into my hands. They are safer there than on your own. I am with you every step of the way. Let us face this day together, with me leading and guiding you.

AUGUST 5ᵀᴴ

Finding Overflow in His Presence

Matthew 6:33

But seek first his kingdom and his righteousness, and all these things will be given to you as well.

The Father is saying, "Spend time with me, beloved. I long to fill you with my presence, anointing your head with oil and making your cup overflow." I will guide you through this day, one step at a time. Many of my children rush ahead, missing the chance to fully experience each moment with me. Slow down and redirect your focus onto me. I desire your full attention, as everything else—your marriage, finances, and family—will align when your heart and mind remain centered on me. Seek the kingdom of God and His righteousness first, and all these things will be added unto you."

AUGUST 6TH

Attuning to the Still Small Voice

John 10:27

My sheep listen to my voice; I know them, and they follow me.

The Father is saying, "Pay close attention to that still, small voice guiding you. It is I, leading you into all truth and moving mountains on your behalf." Be obedient to this voice. Discern whether it is my voice, which brings peace and love, or the enemy's, which introduces fear and chaos. My sheep hear my voice; I know them, and they follow me. You will sense my peace when I speak to you, my beloved. I communicate through the Word of God and others. I am God, and I can do anything. Open your heart to the unknown and seek me diligently.

AUGUST 7ᵀᴴ

Surrendering to Freedom

> Psalm 52:2

You who practice deceit, your tongue plots destruction; it is like a sharpened razor.

> Galatians 5:16-26

So I say, walk by the Spirit, and you will not gratify the desires of the flesh. ¹⁷ For the flesh desires what is contrary to the Spirit, and the Spirit what is contrary to the flesh. They are in conflict with each other, so that you are not to do whatever you want. ¹⁸ But if you are led by the Spirit, you are not under the law. ¹⁹ The acts of the flesh are obvious: sexual immorality, impurity, and debauchery; ²⁰ idolatry and witchcraft; hatred, discord, jealousy, fits of rage, selfish ambition, dissensions, factions²¹, and envy; drunkenness, orgies, and the like. I warn you, as I did before, that those who live like this will not inherit the kingdom of God.²² But the fruit of the Spirit is love, joy, peace, forbearance, kindness, goodness, faithfulness, ²³ gentleness and self-control. Against such things, there is no law. ²⁴ Those who belong to Christ Jesus have crucified the flesh with its passions and desires. ²⁵ Since we live by the Spirit, let us keep in step with the Spirit. ²⁶ Let us not become conceited, provoking, and envying each other.

The Father is saying, "Surrender your life to me—your ways, habits, and insecurities." I desire to transform your thoughts and free you in every area of your life. Many of my children are troubled by intrusive and racing thoughts, often stemming from rebellion and agreement with the enemy's lies. Today, renounce all lies and disassociate from the enemy's deception. Surrender to my will. Take authority over the spirit of deception and cast it down in the name of Jesus. Speak aloud, 'I come out of every agreement with the enemy. I break every word curse spoken over me and my family in Jesus' name. I renounce all deception and rebuke every lie from the pit of hell.' I am setting you free now in Jesus' name.

AUGUST 8ᵀᴴ

Removing Hindrances to Your Relationship with God

Exodus 34:14

Do not worship any other god, for the Lord, whose name is Jealous, is a jealous God.

Exodus 6:7

I will take you as my own people, and I will be your God. Then you will know that I am the Lord your God, who brought you out from under the yoke of the Egyptians.

The Father is saying, "Remove everything that hinders your relationship with me." If people or habits pull you into a cycle of sin, release them to me today. These things are merely obstacles to our closeness. I desire your full attention and commitment. I am a jealous God. Often, my children place other things above me, allowing them to become idols. Today, repent for any way you have put something else before me. Remember, I am your God, and you shall worship no other. I am the Lord, whose name is Jealous, and I am a jealous God.

AUGUST 9ᵀᴴ

Divine Acceleration for Your Promises

Isaiah 43:19

See, I am doing a new thing! Now it springs up; do you not perceive it? I am making a way in the wilderness and streams in the wasteland.

2 Chronicles 26:15-17

In Jerusalem he made devices invented for use on the towers and on the corner defenses so that soldiers could shoot arrows and hurl large stones from the walls. His fame spread far and wide, for he was greatly helped until he became powerful. ¹⁶ But after Uzziah became powerful, his pride led to his downfall. He was unfaithful to the Lord his God and entered the temple of the Lord to burn incense on the altar of incense. ¹⁷ Azariah the priest, with eighty other courageous priests of the Lord followed him in.

The Father is saying, "I am preparing to propel you forward in your ministry, finances, and relationships" What you could not accomplish on your own, I will achieve for you. What might take years, I will bring about overnight. Do not be concerned with the doubts of others or those who question you. You have stood firm, trusted my words, and immediately followed my instructions. Because of your faithfulness, I am about to launch you into the fulfillment of your prayers. This journey has been challenging; you have fasted, made sacrifices, and let go of relationships for my sake. Your unwavering trust and humility have brought you to this moment. Now, watch as I do a new thing. I am making a way in the wilderness and creating streams in the wasteland. Receive this in the spirit, for I am moving powerfully in your life, in Jesus' name.

AUGUST 10TH

Ever-Present Love

> John 14:26

But the Advocate, the Holy Spirit, whom the Father will send in my name, will teach you all things and will remind you of everything I have said to you.

The Father is saying that He is with you, always. From the moment you wake to when you lay down, His presence surrounds you. Though loneliness may sometimes feel overwhelming, remember you are never truly alone. The Holy Spirit, sent to guide you, will lead you into all truth. Do not rely solely on your feelings or emotions; instead, allow the Holy Spirit to empower and enable you to accomplish what you cannot do alone. The Holy Spirit, sent by the Father in Jesus' name, will teach and remind you of His words. Remember, His love for you is unwavering and eternal. You are supported and cherished—never forgotten, never abandoned.

AUGUST 11ᵀᴴ

Renewed Strength in Trials

Luke 10:19

I have given you authority to trample on snakes and scorpions and to overcome all the power of the enemy; nothing will harm you.

2 Corinthians 4:8-12

We are hard pressed on every side, but not crushed; perplexed, but not in despair; ⁹ persecuted, but not abandoned; struck down, but not destroyed. ¹⁰ We always carry around in our body the death of Jesus, so that the life of Jesus may also be revealed in our body. ¹¹ For we who are alive are always being given over to death for Jesus' sake so that his life may also be revealed in our mortal body. ¹² So then, death is at work in us, but life is at work in you.

The Father is saying that even though we may feel hard-pressed on every side, we are not crushed; perplexed, but not in despair; persecuted, yet not abandoned; struck down, but not destroyed. Despite outward struggles, we are being renewed inwardly day by day. When you feel weak, remember that both your spirit and the Holy Spirit provide strength. In moments of intense mental and emotional attack, know that you have been given power and authority to overcome any threat. Stand firm, knowing the enemy's power is limited to what you allow. Choose truth over lies and seek the Holy Spirit's guidance to reveal deception. Have faith, stand firm, and remember that the Father is with you, surrounding you with His unwavering presence. He will never leave you.

AUGUST 12TH

Divine Protection and Preparation

Genesis 24:31

"Come, you who are blessed by the Lord," he said. "Why are you standing out here? I have prepared the house and a place for the camels."

Isaiah 43:2

When you pass through the waters, I will be with you, and when you pass through the rivers, they will not sweep over you. When you walk through the fire, you will not be burned; the flames will not set you ablaze.

The Father is saying that He is clearing away the clutter from your life, including removing individuals who no longer serve a purpose. This process is not about rejection but protection and preparation for the future He has in store for you. Some people cannot go where He is leading you; their presence would hinder your journey. You have asked for His will to be done, even when it means facing painful truths, and this is His will. Although not everyone will understand, trust that He comprehends your pain and is healing you. He is removing the arrows the enemy has aimed at you, ensuring you are protected and restored in the name of Jesus.

AUGUST 13TH

Focused Through the Fiery Trials

Psalm 91:5

You will not fear the terror of night,

nor the arrow that flies by day,

1 Peter 4:12

Dear friends, do not be surprised at the fiery ordeal that has come on you to test you as though something strange were happening to you.

The Father is saying that He wants you to understand that when fiery trials come to test you, they are not to be seen as something strange or unusual. Hardships and trials are a part of the journey, but your focus should remain steadfast on Him. Refocus your mind and ask the Holy Spirit to align your life with His will, restoring order in the name of Jesus. The Lord desires your full attention, with all eyes on Him. He goes before you, beside you, and surrounds you with His protection. His angels are encamped around you, ensuring your safety. There is no need to fear the terrors of the night or the arrows that fly by day.

AUGUST 14ᵀᴴ

Never Alone in the Fire

Psalm 56:8

Record my misery; list my tears on your scroll— are they not in your record?

James 1:2-4

Consider it pure joy, my brothers and sisters,[a] whenever you face trials of many kinds, ³ because you know that the testing of your faith produces perseverance. ⁴ Let perseverance finish its work so that you may be mature and complete, not lacking anything.

The Father is saying that no matter how many trials you face, you will never face them alone. Your Abba is right there with you in the midst of every challenge. Instead of looking to the right or the left, keep your gaze upward and remember that your help comes from the Lord. Even when people fail you or walk away, know that the love of your Father is unwavering. He will never leave or forsake you. He sees every tear you shed and every moment you feel overlooked. Your Father in Heaven has not forgotten you; He has recorded each of your sorrows and collected your tears. Consider it pure joy when you face various trials, knowing that these tests of faith produce perseverance. Allow perseverance to work fully in you so you may become mature and complete, lacking nothing.

August 15th

Victory Through Every Battle

Luke 6:27-28

"But to you who are listening, I say: Love your enemies, do good to those who hate you, ²⁸ bless those who curse you, pray for those who mistreat you.

Romans 1:1-2

Paul, a servant of Christ Jesus, called to be an apostle and set apart for the gospel of God— ² the gospel he promised beforehand through his prophets in the Holy Scriptures.

The Father is saying He understands that you are facing battles unseen by others, but He is fully aware of them. He assures you every battle has been won, even if you don't see it yet. By faith, trust in the victory you have in Jesus' name. There is triumph in your family, finances, and every struggle you face. These trials are shaping your character and teaching you resilience. In your pain, remember that God sees you and understands the enemy's attacks. Don't let these struggles define you or deter you from your calling. Pain can drive you to seek God more deeply and align with His purpose. You are exactly where He has called you to be. Resist allowing others to influence or contaminate you; forgive those who hurt you instead. Love your enemies, do good to those who hate you, bless those who curse you, and pray for those who mistreat you.

August 16th

Breaking Down Barriers

1 Peter 2:9

But you are a chosen people, a royal priesthood, a holy nation, God's special possession, that you may declare the praises of him who called you out of darkness into his wonderful light.

2 Corinthians 10:5

We demolish arguments and every pretension that sets itself up against the knowledge of God, and we take captive every thought to make it obedient to Christ.

The Father is saying that He invites you to let His presence dismantle the barriers that have long held you back. These barriers may have become so familiar that you begin to accept them as part of who you are, but that is a lie. He is breaking down the barriers of depression and anxiety in your life. You are not called to be bound by these conditions. In Jesus' name, all strongholds of anxiety and depression are being dismantled. When thoughts of defeat arise, take them captive and make them obedient to Christ. Reject every high thought that opposes the knowledge of God. You are not meant to be bound by deceit or enemy tactics. You are a chosen people, a royal priesthood, a holy nation, God's special possession, called to declare His praises and step into His marvelous light.

AUGUST 17ᵀᴴ

Rise Above and Embrace Your Royalty

John 14:6

Jesus answered, "I am the way and the truth and the life. No one comes to the Father except through me.

Luke 6:27-28

"But to you who are listening, I say: Love your enemies, do good to those who hate you, ²⁸ bless those who curse you, pray for those who mistreat you.

The Father is saying that you should rise from depression and challenging situations. It's time to shake off everything the enemy has thrown at you. Remember, you are a child of the King, seated in heavenly places with Him. Your enemies have no power over you; they cannot touch you. When faced with negativity or evil, respond with prayer and forgiveness, for they do not know what they are doing. Your Abba Father calls you by name, inviting you to rise to higher and deeper dimensions. The only path to the Father is through Jesus Christ. He loves you deeply and is proud of you.

AUGUST 18ᵀᴴ

Faithful in the Face of Trials

> Matthew 4:4

Jesus answered, "It is written: 'Man shall not live on bread alone, but on every word that comes from the mouth of God.'"

> Psalm 16:11

You make known to me the path of life;

you will fill me with joy in your presence,

with eternal pleasures at your right hand.

The Father is saying that you should continue to show up, serve, and remain faithful. He sees your steadfastness, even when many have walked away. Though difficult, remember that the victory is already secured in Christ Jesus. He witnessed your betrayals and the abandonment by loved ones. You have not given up despite the challenges, for the Spirit of God within you is stronger than any obstacle. No devil or person can stop you from fulfilling your divine calling. It is written that man lives not by bread alone but by every word from God. Meditate on His Word and let His holy presence fill your mind and heart, saturating you completely, from head to toe, in Jesus' name.

AUGUST 19ᵀᴴ

The Strength for Your Journey

Isaiah 46:4

Even to your old age and gray hairs I am he, I am he who will sustain you. I have made you, and I will carry you; I will sustain you, and I will rescue you.

Isaiah 43:2

When you pass through the waters, I will be with you, and when you pass through the rivers, they will not sweep over you. When you walk through the fire, you will not be burned; the flames will not set you ablaze.

The Father is saying that He is your strength and is guides you through this journey. You are not alone; He is carrying you every step of the way. When you have asked for strength, He has been providing it. On days when even daily tasks seem overwhelming, and you cry out for His help, He has heard your pleas. He has been holding you through the challenges, doubts, and pain. Even when you faced seemingly insurmountable obstacles, His support helped you persevere. Remember, He is always with you as your God, protector, and loving Father.

AUGUST 20ᵀᴴ

Trust in My Unseen Work

2 Corinthians 5:7

For we live by faith, not by sight.

Psalms 32:8

I will instruct you and teach you in the way you should go;

I will counsel you with my loving eye on you.

The Father is saying that you should begin this day by saying thanks for all you have done and will do. I am continuously at work in your life, even when you do not see or feel it. This is why I instruct My children to walk by faith, not sight. Many give up when they do not see immediate changes in their circumstances. Ask the Holy Spirit to open your spiritual eyes so you can perceive what I am doing in your life. Remember, you have not yet seen or heard the fullness of My work. Trust in Me, and do not be swayed by your feelings or emotions. Let the Spirit of the living God guide you, and I will direct your path.

AUGUST 21ST

Finding Rest in the Secret Place

> Exodus 20:3

You shall have no other gods before[a] me.

> Chronicles 16:11

Look to the Lord and his strength;

seek his face always.

The Father is saying that you should unwind from the pressures of daily life and spend time with Him in the secret place. He desires to speak with you and provide guidance. You may have been seeking answers to life's challenges and how to handle various circumstances. His answer is simple: trust in Him alone. Many turn to people, money, and material possessions to cope, but these are worldly and can become idols. Remember, He is the Lord your God who delivered you from bondage. No other gods should come before Him. Continue to trust Him with all your heart, soul, and mind.

AUGUST 22ND

Through Each Day

> Proverbs 4:12

When you walk, your steps will not be hampered;

when you run, you will not stumble.

> 2 Corinthians 5:7

For we live by faith, not by sight.

> Psalm 18:29

He brought me out into a spacious place;

he rescued me because he delighted in me.

The Father is saying He wants you to know He is leading and guiding you, so there is no need for doubt. Do not let distractions interfere with your journey. While you may not fully understand His work in your life now, you will gain clarity in time. This path may be challenging, but you can overcome any obstacle together. Your commitment to Him will bring success in all your endeavors. Focus on living one day and taking one step at a time. Although planning is important, getting ahead too quickly can lead to frustration. Embrace the peace He offers and trust that you are securely held in His hands.

AUGUST 23ᴿᴰ

Moving Forward in Faith

John 4:34

"My food," said Jesus, "is to do the will of him who sent me and to finish his work.

Genesis 19:17-26

As soon as they had brought them out, one of them said, "Flee for your lives! Don't look back, and don't stop anywhere in the plain! Flee to the mountains, or you will be swept away!" ¹⁸ But Lot said to them, "No, my Lords, please! ¹⁹ Your servant has found favor in your eyes, and you have shown great kindness to me in sparing my life. But I can't flee to the mountains; this disaster will overtake me, and I'll die. ²⁰ Look, here is a town near enough to run to, and it is small. Let me flee to it—it is very small, isn't it? Then my life will be spared."

²¹ He said to him, "Very well, I will grant this request too; I will not overthrow the town you speak of. ²² But flee there quickly because I cannot do anything until you reach it." (That is why the town was called Zoar.) ²³ By the time Lot reached Zoar, the sun had risen over the land. ²⁴ Then the Lord rained down burning sulfur on Sodom and Gomorrah—from the Lord out of the heavens. ²⁵ Thus, he overthrew those cities and the entire plain, destroying all those living in the cities—and also the vegetation in the land. ²⁶ But Lot's wife looked back, and she became a pillar of salt.

The Father is saying that He advises you not to look back like Lot's wife, who became a pillar of salt when she turned to the past. Just as He led you out of Egypt and away from past struggles, He urges you not to return to old habits, places, or relationships merely for comfort. What He has planned for you is far greater than what you leave behind. Remember, those who cling to their old ways will lose them, but those who embrace change will find true preservation. Trust that He is in control, guiding you to places beyond your imagination and bringing the right people into your life. He is replacing the old with something better. Just as Jesus said, His purpose was to do the will of the Father and complete His work.

AUGUST 24ᵀᴴ

Embracing Your Light

Isaiah 43:1-4

But now, this is what the Lord says— he who created you, Jacob, he who formed you, Israel:

"Do not fear, for I have redeemed you; I have summoned you by name; you are mine. ² When you pass through the waters, I will be with you; and when you pass through the rivers, they will not sweep over you. When you walk through the fire, you will not be burned; the flames will not set you ablaze. ³ For I am the Lord your God, the Holy One of Israel, your Savior; I give Egypt for your ransom, Cush and Seba in your stead. ⁴ Since you are precious and honored in my sight, and because I love you, I will give people in exchange for you, nations in exchange for your life.

The Father is saying that the light shines in the darkness, and the darkness cannot overcome it. He has called you to be that light in this world. You are set apart and appointed by Him. As the Lord who created and formed you says, do not fear; He has redeemed and called you by name. You belong to Him, and He makes no mistakes. Remember that God qualifies you, not others, even if you don't always feel qualified. He is always with you, guiding and supporting you every step of the way. You are precious in His sight, and He has chosen you for a purpose.

August 25th

Freedom from Condemnation

Romans 8:1

Therefore, there is now no condemnation for those who are in Christ Jesus,

2 Corinthians 5:17

Therefore, if anyone is in Christ, the new creation has come: The old has gone, the new is here!

The Father is saying that there is no condemnation for those in Christ Jesus. All past mistakes, whether from yesterday, months ago, or even years ago, have been forgiven. If you have repented, those sins are gone. When feelings of guilt from past errors arise, take authority over them and cast them down in Jesus' name. His name holds power over every demon, sickness, and disease. You are a new creation in Christ Jesus, and He is with you always. He will never leave you or forsake you.

August 26th

Unchanging Guidance

Romans 6:19

I am using an example from everyday life because of your human limitations. Just as you used to offer yourselves as slaves to impurity and to ever-increasing wickedness, so now offer yourselves as slaves to righteousness leading to holiness.

Hebrews 13:8

Jesus Christ is the same yesterday and today and forever.

The Father is saying that He is the same yesterday, today, and forever—He never changes. While your thoughts and emotions may fluctuate, His constancy remains. Allow the Spirit of God to lead you as He speaks to you in ways that address your human limitations. As you once yielded your body to impurity and lawlessness, dedicate yourself to righteousness and sanctification. Though the maturing process may be uncomfortable, remember that He never promised ease but offers His steadfast presence. Reach out for His hand, and He will guide you through every challenge. Listen to His still, small voice and be obedient, knowing you can overcome anything together.

AUGUST 27ᵀᴴ

Finding Joy in Trials

> Proverbs 16:9

In their hearts, humans plan their course, but the Lord establishes their steps.

> Isaiah 40:31

but those who hope in the Lord will renew their strength. They will soar on wings like eagles; they will run and not grow weary; they will walk and not be faint.

The Father is saying that you should not be surprised by the fiery trials you face, as though something unusual is happening. Instead, rejoice that you are sharing in Christ's sufferings, knowing that you will also share in His glory when it is revealed. He is with you in every trial, storm, drought, or sickness. Though you may not see immediate results, believe in miracles and healing. Just because it hasn't happened yet doesn't mean it won't. Trust in God's perfect timing, and keep your faith and obedience steadfast. His timing is always perfect, and He remains with you through it all.

AUGUST 28TH

Trusting the Unseen Path

Philippians 2:14-15

Do everything without grumbling or arguing, ¹⁵ so that you may become blameless and pure, "children of God without fault in a warped and crooked generation." Then you will shine among them like stars in the sky

Matthew 22:37-40

Jesus replied: "'Love the Lord your God with all your heart and with all your soul and with all your mind.' ³⁸ This is the first and greatest commandment. ³⁹ And the second is like it: 'Love your neighbor as yourself.' ⁴⁰ All the Law and the Prophets hang on these two commandments."

The Father is saying not to doubt His work in your life. He is making a way where none seemed possible. Many of His children falter when they don't immediately see His promises fulfilled or experience the healing He has assured. Faith is crucial; without it, it is impossible to please God. Will you trust Him even when you don't see results? Will you obey His guidance even when it feels uncomfortable or illogical? Be attentive to His still, small voice, and trust Him with all your heart, mind, and soul. Shift your focus away from complaints, surrender fully to Him, and serve with a heart aligned with His will.

AUGUST 29ᵀᴴ

Embracing Your Unique Journey

John 10:10

The thief comes only to steal and kill and destroy; I have come that they may have life and have it to the full.

Zechariah 3:2

The Lord said to Satan, "The Lord rebuke you, Satan! The Lord, who has chosen Jerusalem, rebuke you! Is not this man a burning stick snatched from the fire?"

The Father is saying not to diminish your journey or compare it with others. Each of His children is on a unique path, but all are walking the same journey with Him. When the spirit of comparison tempts you, take authority over it and cast it away in the name of Jesus. Avoid falling into the enemy's trap, as the evil one seeks to use anything to hinder you. Remember, the thief comes only to steal, kill, and destroy, but Jesus came to give life abundantly. When faced with temptation, rebuke the enemy's tactics and speak the Word of God over your life.

AUGUST 30TH

Choosing Your Path

Revelation 3:15-18

I know your deeds, that you are neither cold nor hot. I wish you were either one or the other! ¹⁶ So, because you are lukewarm—neither hot nor cold—I am about to spit you out of my mouth. ¹⁷ You say, 'I am rich; I have acquired wealth and do not need a thing.' But you do not realize that you are wretched, pitiful, poor, blind, and naked. ¹⁸ I counsel you to buy from me gold refined in the fire, so you can become rich, and white clothes to wear, so you can cover your shameful nakedness; and salve to put on your eyes, so you can see.

Revelation 2:1-7

"To the angel of the church in Ephesus, write:

These are the words of him who holds the seven stars in his right hand and walks among the seven golden lampstands. ² I know your deeds, your hard work, and your perseverance. I know that you cannot tolerate wicked people, that you have tested those who claim to be apostles but are not and have found them false. ³ You have persevered and have endured hardships for my name and have not grown weary. ⁴ Yet I hold this against you: You have forsaken the love you had at first. ⁵ Consider how far you have fallen! Repent and do the things you did at first. If you do not repent, I will come to you and remove your lampstand from its place. ⁶ But you have this in your favor: You hate the practices of the Nicolaitans, which I also hate. ⁷ Whoever has ears, let them hear what the Spirit says to the churches. To the one who is victorious, I will give the right to eat from the tree of life, which is in the paradise of God.

The Father is saying He needs a clear commitment. He is grieved by actions that try to straddle the line between the world and Him. This notion of having one foot in each realm is a lie from the enemy and a form of deception. Repent and turn away from these wicked ways. Do not delay your return to God, thinking you have time to change later. The Lord prefers you to be fully committed, either hot or cold, rather than lukewarm. Being indifferent or half-hearted is unacceptable. He warns that if you remain lukewarm, you risk being cast aside. As He prepares to return, turn away from evil, repent, and renew your commitment to Him. Remember your first love, repent, and return to the works you once did. If not, He will remove your lampstand from its place.

August 31ST

Embracing Unlimited Favor

1 Corinthians 14:33

For God is not a God of disorder but of peace—as in all the congregations of the Lord's people.

The Father is saying that He promises you unlimited favor in everything you do. His favor will touch all your actions and words. When you speak, He will provide the words you need. Do not worry about what to say or do; He can work wonders beyond your imagination. Trust in His ability to accomplish great things in and through you. Avoid letting the enemy sow seeds of doubt and confusion. Remember, God is not the author of confusion but of peace, providing clarity and tranquility to His beloved.

SEPTEMBER 1ST

Prioritizing Christ Above All

> John 8:44

You belong to your father, the devil, and you want to carry out your father's desires. He was a murderer from the beginning, not holding to the truth, for there is no truth in him. When he lies, he speaks his native language, for he is a liar and the father of lies.

The Father is saying that His mission was not to bring peace but a sword, setting man against father and daughter against mother. To follow Him, you must prioritize your relationship with Him above all others, even if it means losing friends or family. Some have departed from your life because they rejected Him, the way, the truth, and the life. Do not let the enemy manipulate your emotions or use these losses against you. Ask the Holy Spirit for increased discernment to distinguish between the wheat, representing the children of God, and the tares, representing those of evil. Stay focused on Christ alone, and remember that you are accepted into the kingdom of God, not rejected.

SEPTEMBER 2ND

Overcoming Fear and Embracing Your Purpose

Isaiah 43:4-6

Since you are precious and honored in my sight,
and because I love you,
I will give people in exchange for you,
nations in exchange for your life.
⁵ Do not be afraid, for I am with you;
I will bring your children from the east
and gather you from the west.
⁶ I will say to the north, 'Give them up!'
and to the south, 'Do not hold them back.'
Bring my sons from afar
and my daughters from the ends of the earth—

The Father is saying that He expects you to teach new disciples to follow all His commands, assuring you of His presence until the end of the age. When fear arises unexpectedly, take authority and cast it away in Jesus' name. Remember, you are a soldier in a spiritual battle, not a physical one. Your weapons have the divine power to demolish strongholds and arguments against the knowledge of God. Capture every thought and make it obedient to Christ. Seek the Holy Spirit's strength to bolster your faith and courage in every area of your life. Reject feelings of unworthiness, for you are esteemed and loved by God. He values you so greatly that He would exchange others for your life. Do not fear; He is with you and will gather you and your loved ones from every direction.

SEPTEMBER 3ʳᵈ

Following God's Guidance

Deuteronomy 12:24

You must not eat the blood; pour it out on the ground like water.

Psalm 32:8

I will instruct you and teach you in the way you should go; I will counsel you with my loving eye on you.

The Father is saying He will call you to obey all His commands carefully. Show your love for Him by walking in His ways and clinging to Him, listening intently to His still, small voice. He is guiding you on the right path. Keep your focus on Him, avoiding distractions and doubts. When you question whether you hear His voice, know it is the Lord speaking. He will instruct and teach you, offering counsel with His loving eye. Trust His guidance and remain steadfast in your journey with Him.

SEPTEMBER 4TH

Declaring Your Trust in God

> Proverbs 3:18
>
> She is a tree of life to those who take hold of her;
>
> those who hold her fast will be blessed.

The Father is saying that He invites you to affirm your trust in Him openly. When you feel anxious, declare, "I trust in You, Lord." By speaking these words and believing them in your heart, you declare faith in Jesus' name. Trust Him even when you don't see immediate results or the fulfillment of your prayers. Remember, He will never leave you. Reject any thoughts or lies suggesting otherwise, casting them away in Jesus' name. Surrender every aspect of your life to Him, for your life is better in His hands than your own. Understand that relying on your strength can lead to pride. Repent of any pride and embrace His strength, knowing He desires to guide and support you according to His will.

SEPTEMBER 5ᵀᴴ

Seeking God's Guidance Daily

> Proverbs 3:5-6

Trust in the Lord with all your heart and lean not on your own understanding; ⁶ in all your ways submit to him, and he will make your paths straight.

The Father is saying you must diligently seek His face every day. As the omnipresent God of Abraham, Isaac, and Jacob, He is always with you, working in your life visibly and behind the scenes. Be thankful for all He has done and continues to do. In moments of stillness, remember that He is God and is working everything out for your good. Trust Him with all your heart, and don't rely solely on your understanding. Acknowledge Him in all your ways, and He will direct your paths. He promises to guide you in truth, ensuring you never go astray.

SEPTEMBER 6ᵀᴴ

You Are Seen and Known

Psalm 66:11

You brought us into prison and laid burdens on our backs.

Jeremiah 1:5

"Before I formed you in the womb, I knew you; before you were born, I set you apart; I appointed you as a prophet to the nations."

1 Corinthians 2:14

The person without the Spirit does not accept the things that come from the Spirit of God but considers them foolishness and cannot understand them because they are discerned only through the Spirit.

The Father is saying that He sees you, beloved. You are never alone, even in times of betrayal and misunderstanding. Forgive those who have wronged you, for they do not understand what they are doing. You have made great progress, and I am proud of how far you have come. Do not let the lack of understanding from others bring you down. Natural persons do not comprehend the things of the Spirit; they are spiritually discerned and may seem foolish to the world. It's okay to be misunderstood. What truly matters is that I know you. I created you before you were born, set you apart, and appointed you for a purpose. You are mine, and I am yours.

SEPTEMBER 7TH

Seek My Guidance in All Things

1 Corinthians 45:33

Matthew 18:15-20

"If your brother or sister[a] sins,[b] go and point out their fault, just between the two of you. If they listen to you, you have won them over. ¹⁶ But if they will not listen, take one or two others along, so that 'every matter may be established by the testimony of two or three witnesses.'[c] ¹⁷ If they still refuse to listen, tell it to the church; and if they refuse to listen even to the church, treat them as you would a pagan or a tax collector. ¹⁸ "Truly I tell you, whatever you bind on earth will be[d] bound in heaven, and whatever you loose on earth will be[e] loosed in heaven. ¹⁹ "Again, truly I tell you that if two of you on earth agree about anything they ask for, it will be done for them by my Father in heaven. ²⁰ For where two or three gather in my name, there am I with them."

Colossians 4:6

Let your conversation be always full of grace, seasoned with salt, so that you may know how to answer everyone.

The Father is saying to approach everything you hear with discernment. Always bring your concerns and feelings to Me first. By doing this, you will find that the burdens trying to attach themselves to you will quickly dissipate. Use discernment when responding to others and listening to their words. My Holy Spirit will guide you and reveal what you need to know. If you've asked me to show you the true nature of certain people, I am doing so, but remember to pray for them rather than judge them. It's okay if the truth isn't what you expected; continue to pray and maintain a safe distance if needed. Remember, bad company can corrupt good character.

SEPTEMBER 8ᵀᴴ

Trust in the Promise Keeper

> Psalm 102:16-17

For the Lord will rebuild Zion
and appear in his glory.
¹⁷ He will respond to the prayer of the destitute;
he will not despise their plea.

> Thessalonians 5:23-24

May God himself, the God of peace, sanctify you through and through. May your whole spirit, soul, and body be kept blameless at the coming of our Lord Jesus Christ. ²⁴ The one who calls you is faithful, and he will do it.

The Father is saying that the Lord will rebuild Zion and reveal His glory. He hears the prayers of the destitute and does not overlook their pleas. I hear your cries for help and know you have been awake through many restless nights. I am working on your behalf, even when you cannot see it. I am always moving things and orchestrating changes behind the scenes. Your part is to trust and obey Me. Regardless of what you observe around you, trust Me when it doesn't make sense, in times of discomfort, and even when the promises seem unfulfilled. Just because you haven't seen the promise come to fruition yet doesn't mean I am not fulfilling it. I am a promise keeper, not a man who lies. I am a faithful Father and a mighty God who can achieve the impossible—believe and have faith.

SEPTEMBER 9TH

I Am With You

Ephesians 1:13-14

And you also were included in Christ when you heard the message of truth, the gospel of your salvation. When you believed, you were marked in him with a seal, the promised Holy Spirit, [14] who is a deposit guaranteeing our inheritance until the redemption of those who are God's possession—to the praise of his glory.

Galatians 6:9

Let us not become weary in doing good, for at the proper time we will reap a harvest if we do not give up.

The Father is saying, "I am with you in every step you take." Do not be swayed by the turmoil around you. Stay rooted where you are; I am present in every move you make. When you lack the words to pray, I will provide the extra push you need. The Holy Spirit will intercede with groans and prayers beyond your understanding. I will give you the words and the strength when you feel too weak to continue. I know the battle has been long, and you are weary, but remember, I am here. You have been asking where I am—here I am. I am calling you, anointing you, and filling you with my Spirit. I have sealed you and paid the price for you.

SEPTEMBER 10TH

Embraced by Everlasting Love

Jeremiah 31:3

The Lord appeared to us in the past, saying: "I have loved you with an everlasting love; I have drawn you with unfailing kindness.

Romans 8:1

Therefore, there is now no condemnation for those who are in Christ Jesus,

1 John 1:9

If we confess our sins, he is faithful and just and will forgive us our sins and purify us from all unrighteousness.

The Father is saying, "Beloved, I want you to know how deeply I love you. My love for you is everlasting, and with loving kindness, I have drawn you near and remain faithful to you. I have not forgotten you or written you off." Even if you feel overlooked, remember I will never leave nor forsake you. If mistakes have led to feelings of condemnation, I rebuke that spirit in Jesus' name. Condemnation comes from the enemy, but conviction is from the Holy Spirit. There is no condemnation for those in Christ Jesus. Spend time with me, and let my presence fill and renew you. Everyone makes mistakes, but do not let them weigh you down. Instead, let my grace strengthen you. You are forgiven and chosen, my beloved.

SEPTEMBER 11ᵀᴴ

Training in Divine Sovereignty

Revelation 12:1-12

A great sign appeared in heaven: a woman clothed with the sun, with the moon under her feet and a crown of twelve stars on her head. ² She was pregnant and cried out in pain as she was about to give birth. ³ Then another sign appeared in heaven: an enormous red dragon with seven heads, ten horns, and seven crowns on its heads. ⁴ Its tail swept a third of the stars out of the sky and flung them to the earth. The dragon stood in front of the woman who was about to give birth so that it might devour her child the moment he was born. ⁵ She gave birth to a son, a male child, who "will rule all the nations with an iron scepter."[a] And her child was snatched up to God and to his throne. ⁶ The woman fled into the wilderness to a place prepared for her by God, where she might be taken care of for 1,260 days. ⁷ Then war broke out in heaven. Michael and his angels fought against the dragon, and the dragon and his angels fought back.⁸ But he was not strong enough, and they lost their place in heaven. ⁹ The great dragon was hurled down—that ancient serpent called the devil, or Satan, who leads the whole world astray. He was hurled to the earth, and his angels with him. ¹⁰ Then I heard a loud voice in heaven say: "Now have come the salvation and the power and the kingdom of our God, and the authority of his Messiah. For the accuser of our brothers and sisters, who accuses them before our God day and night, has been hurled down. ¹¹ They triumphed over him by the blood of the Lamb and by the word of their testimony; they did not love their lives so much as to shrink from death. ¹² Therefore rejoice, you heavens and you who dwell in them! But woe to the earth and the sea because the devil has gone down to you! He is filled with fury because he knows that his time is short."

Job 22:28

What you decide on will be done, and light will shine on your ways.

Ezekiel 37:1-10

The hand of the Lord was on me, and he brought me out by the Spirit of the Lord and set me in the middle of a valley; it was full of bones. ² He led me back and forth among them, and I saw a great many bones on the floor of the valley, bones that were very dry. ³ He asked me, "Son of man, can these bones live?" I said, "Sovereign Lord, you alone know." ⁴ Then he said to me, "Prophesy to these bones and say to them, 'Dry bones, hear the word of the Lord! ⁵ This is what the Sovereign Lord says to these bones: I will make breath[a] enter you, and you will come to life. ⁶ I will attach tendons to you and make flesh come upon you and cover you with skin; I will put breath in you, and you will come to life. Then you will know that I am the Lord.'" ⁷ So I prophesied as I was commanded. And as I was prophesying, there was a noise, a rattling sound, and the bones came together, bone to bone. ⁸ I looked, and tendons and flesh appeared on them, and skin covered them, but there was no breath in them. ⁹ Then he said to me, "Prophesy to the breath; prophesy, son of man, and say to it, 'This is what the Sovereign Lord says: Come, breath, from the four winds and breathe into these slain, that they may live.'" ¹⁰ So I prophesied as he commanded me, and breath entered them; they came to life and stood up on their feet—a vast army.

The Father is saying, "I am guiding you in the way you should go, laying down the principles of my sovereignty. I am supreme in all things, the Father, Son, and Holy Spirit, holding all power and authority." When you believe in my power, I work through and in you. In facing challenges, obstacles, and conflicts, be still and know I am God. Take authority over any opposition and bind it; you are battle-ready as a soldier in my kingdom. Know that you have already won in your finances, life, and children's lives because Christ lives in you. Victory has been secured by the blood of Jesus. Declare and decree this victory over every situation, prophesying over yourself and your family, for the living God dwells within you.

SEPTEMBER 12ᵀᴴ

Rising to the Mountaintop

Exodus 24:12

The Lord said to Moses, "Come up to me on the mountain and stay here, and I will give you the tablets of stone with the law and commandments I have written for their instruction."

Matthew 9:17

Neither do people pour new wine into old wineskins. If they do, the skins will burst, the wine will run out, and the wineskins will be ruined. No, they pour new wine into new wineskins, and both are preserved."

The Father is saying, "I see you, even when you feel unseen. I am calling you to rise higher, to come up to the mountaintop with me. I want to share much with you, to fill and saturate you with my presence. You are my beloved, and I am well pleased with your faithfulness."

Despite the long battles and your reluctance to rise, you have returned to the assignment I gave you. I want to speak to you just as I called Moses to the mountain to receive the stone tablets. I am preparing to pour new wine into you, my beloved. Come closer, for there is so much I wish to reveal and bestow upon you.

SEPTEMBER 13TH

Surrender and Worship

Matthew 11:28-30

"Come to me, all you who are weary and burdened, and I will give you rest. ²⁹ Take my yoke upon you and learn from me, for I am gentle and humble in heart, and you will find rest for your souls. ³⁰ For my yoke is easy, and my burden is light."

Deuteronomy 6:4-9

Hear, O Israel: The Lord our God, the Lord is one.[a] ⁵ Love the Lord your God with all your heart and with all your soul and with all your strength. ⁶ These commandments that I give you today are to be on your hearts. ⁷ Impress them on your children. Talk about them when you sit at home and when you walk along the road, when you lie down, and when you get up. ⁸ Tie them as symbols on your hands and bind them on your foreheads. ⁹ Write them on the doorframes of your houses and on your gates.

The Father is saying, "Worship me, for I am worthy of all praise, even if things don't appear to be moving as you expect. In the mighty name of Jesus, I am moving mountains and making changes in your life." Everything works together for your good because I love and have chosen you. You did not choose me; I chose you. As a chosen generation, worship the King of kings and the Lord of Lords. Surrender your situation and any family concerns to me. Listen and obey my still, small voice. I know what is best for you. If you struggle to release your burdens, ask me for more grace; my grace is sufficient. I am the God of grace and mercy, which is always better in my hands than in yours. Lay your burdens down at my feet today, and let my presence heal your beloved heart.

SEPTEMBER 14ᵀᴴ

Embrace the Small Steps

> Matthew 21:22

If you believe, you will receive whatever you ask for in prayer."

> Luke 1:37

For no word from God will ever fail."

> Romans 10:17

Consequently, faith comes from hearing the message, and the message is heard through the word about Christ.

The Father is saying, "Count every bit of progress, and don't underestimate the value of small steps." Each step of faith you take brings you closer to your destiny. Even if it seems things aren't going in your favor, know that everything is unfolding according to my plan. Surrender your will and emotions to me today. Many of my children are guided by their feelings rather than the Holy Spirit. Ask the Holy Spirit to align your emotions with the Word of God. Trust that I am at work in your life, bringing everything into order. I love you deeply and desire what is best for you even more than you do."

SEPTEMBER 15TH

Moving Forward with Confidence

> Isaiah 43:19

See, I am doing a new thing! Now it springs up; do you not perceive it? I am making a way in the wilderness and streams in the wasteland.

> 2 Peter 3:9

The Lord is not slow in keeping his promise, as some understand slowness. Instead, he is patient with you, not wanting anyone to perish, but everyone to come to repentance.

The Father is saying it is time to close the door on your past and break free from all bondage. Move forward from the situations that hold you back, knowing I am with you every step of the way. No enemy is too great for me; we will overcome every giant together. I am a mighty God, and every challenge you face is nothing compared to my power. I am replacing what is counterfeit with what is real—bringing you people who will truly support and uplift you.

Let go of old relationships and circumstances that no longer serve you, and trust me to bring you what is best. Pray for those who have wronged you, for my mercy and grace also extend to them. Many act out of ignorance, driven by forces they do not understand. I am not slowly fulfilling my promises; I am patient, desiring all to come to repentance. Trust in my plan and recognize that I am doing something new. I am making a way in the wilderness and creating rivers in the desert. Embrace this new beginning with faith and confidence.

SEPTEMBER 16TH

Victory in Christ

> Ephesians 6:11-13
>
> Put on the full armor of God so that you can take your stand against the devil's schemes. ¹² For our struggle is not against flesh and blood, but against the rulers, against the authorities, against the powers of this dark world and against the spiritual forces of evil in the heavenly realms. ¹³ Therefore put on the full armor of God, so that when the day of evil comes, you may be able to stand your ground, and after you have done everything, to stand.

The Father is saying the battle has already been won. Allow me to fight for you. You have been striving independently, leading to exhaustion and burnout. Be still and know that I am your God. The sooner you release your worries and concerns to me, the more effectively I can act on your behalf. Some of you have been facing challenges without the proper armor; how can you expect to prevail when your defenses are unprepared?

Put on the whole armor of God so you can stand firm against the devil's schemes. Discern the enemy's tactics and recognize that our struggle is not against flesh and blood but against principalities, powers, and the rulers of darkness in this age. Remember, you are a warrior in Christ Jesus. Sharpen your sword, and claim the victory already yours in His name.

SEPTEMBER 17TH

Overcoming Every Attack

Matthew 10:14-16

If anyone will not welcome you or listen to your words, leave that home or town and shake the dust off your feet. ¹⁵ Truly, I tell you, it will be more bearable for Sodom and Gomorrah on the day of judgment than for that town.

¹⁶ "I am sending you out like sheep among wolves. Therefore, be as shrewd as snakes and as innocent as doves.

John 8:44

You belong to your father, the devil, and you want to carry out your father's desires. He was a murderer from the beginning, not holding to the truth, for there is no truth in him. When he lies, he speaks his native language, for he is a liar and the father of lies.

The Father is saying, "No weapon formed against you shall prosper, even though the enemy is relentless." He may use family, attack your marriage, or cause discord. Take authority over every assault from the enemy and bind every attack in the mighty name of Jesus.

Remember who you are and who you are in every season. The enemy thrives on playing with your emotions, but deception is a lie. Refuse to be misled any longer. Claim your joy, lift your head, and reengage in the battle. The enemy has toyed with you long enough. Rise, shake off the dust, and continue as a forerunner in the kingdom of God.

SEPTEMBER 18ᵀᴴ

Overcoming the Spirit of Fear

2 Timothy 1:7

For the Spirit God gave us does not make us timid but gives us power, love, and self-discipline.

2 Thessalonians 3:16

Now, may the Lord of peace himself give you peace at all times and in every way. The Lord be with all of you.

The Father is saying, "Do not doubt the promises I have spoken over you." Fear may occasionally arise, but remember, fear is a liar. Take authority over the spirit of fear and cast it back into the abyss in the name of Jesus. Fear is a crippling spirit meant to prevent you from fulfilling your calling.

Do not be deceived, beloved. Rebuke and nullify all demonic assignments against you. I want my children to find rest and supernatural peace in my presence. Do not let the enemy steal what I have freely given. Stand firm against every giant in your life and command it to return to the pit of hell. Continuously seek my presence and my will for your life. I will never let you down.

SEPTEMBER 19TH

Embracing the Fire

Isaiah 43:2

When you pass through the waters, I will be with you, and when you pass through the rivers, they will not sweep over you. When you walk through the fire, you will not be burned; the flames will not set you ablaze.

Ephesians 6:10-11

Finally, be strong in the Lord and in his mighty power. [11] Put on the full armor of God so that you can take your stand against the devil's schemes.

The Father is saying it is time to fast and endure until your trials pass. You will face warfare, but I will be with you throughout. They will not overwhelm you when you pass through the waters; when you go through the rivers, they will not sweep over you. When you walk through the fire, you will not be burned; the flames will not scorch you.

As you come through the fire, you will not carry the scent of smoke but instead emerge as the fire of God, ignited within you. You will stand firm against the enemy, knowing who you are in Christ Jesus. The enemy may try various tactics, but you remain steadfast in worshiping the King of Kings. You are my beloved, a firecracker with whom I am well pleased.

SEPTEMBER 20ᵀᴴ

Positioned for Overflow

1 Thessalonians 3:12

May the Lord make your love increase and overflow for each other and for everyone else, just as ours does for you.

Psalm 65

Praise awaits you, our God, in Zion; to you, our vows will be fulfilled. ² You who answer prayer, to you all people will come. ³ When we were overwhelmed by sins, you forgave our transgressions. ⁴ Blessed are those you choose and bring near to live in your courts! We are filled with the good things of your house, of your holy temple. You answer us with awesome and righteous deeds, God our Savior, the hope of all the ends of the earth and of the farthest seas, ⁶who formed the mountains by your power, having armed yourself with strength, l⁷ who stilled the roaring of the seas, the roaring of their waves, and the turmoil of the nations. ⁸ The whole earth is filled with awe at your wonders; where morning dawns, where evening fades, you call forth songs of joy. ⁹ You care for the land and water it; you enrich it abundantly. The streams of God are filled with water to provide the people with grain, for so you have ordained it. ¹⁰ You drench its furrows and level its ridges; you soften it with showers and bless its crops. ¹¹ You crown the year with your bounty, and your carts overflow with abundance. ¹² The grasslands of the wilderness overflow; the hills are clothed with gladness. ¹³The meadows are covered with flocks, and the valleys are mantled with grain; they shout for joy and sing.

The Father is saying to stand firm on the foundation He has laid for you. I have placed you exactly where I want you, positioning you for the promise I have prepared. I have not forgotten you, and I never will. Despite the changing circumstances and emotions, remember that I am unchanging, the same yesterday, today, and forever.

I am not affected by the things around you or shaken. You are in the perfect place to receive all I have for you. I am preparing to place everything you need right into your lap. Your gifts will increase, and you will experience overflow. Keep me first, and you will find that you are never last. Prepare for abundance; I will fill your lap with more than enough.

SEPTEMBER 21ST

Divine Preparation

Proverbs 3:5-6

Trust in the Lord with all your heart and lean not on your own understanding; **6** in all your ways submit to him, and he will make your paths straight.

The Father is saying, "I am with you. The storm you are enduring will soon pass. Trust in me with all your heart, and do not rely on your own understanding. Acknowledge me in all your ways, and I will make your paths straight." I am preparing you for greater things because you possess greatness within you. What you carry is not ordinary; it is extraordinary and divine, crafted uniquely for you. Though the battle has been long, know that I am with you through every moment—whether you rise up or lie down, I am always by your side.

SEPTEMBER 22ND

Embracing Grace Amidst Resistance

1 Peter 4:12-19

Dear friends, do not be surprised at the fiery ordeal that has come on you to test you, as though something strange were happening to you. ¹³ But rejoice inasmuch as you participate in the sufferings of Christ, so that you may be overjoyed when his glory is revealed. ¹⁴ If you are insulted because of the name of Christ, you are blessed, for the Spirit of glory and of God rests on you. ¹⁵ If you suffer, it should not be as a murderer or thief or any other kind of criminal or even as a meddler. ¹⁶ However, if you suffer as a Christian, do not be ashamed, but praise God that you bear that name. ¹⁷ For it is time for judgment to begin with God's household; and if it begins with us, what will the outcome be for those who do not obey the gospel of God? ¹⁸ And, "If it is hard for the righteous to be saved, what will become of the ungodly and the sinner?" ¹⁹ So then, those who suffer according to God's will should commit themselves to their faithful Creator and continue to do good.

Romans 12:2

Do not conform to the pattern of this world, but be transformed by the renewing of your mind. Then, you will be able to test and approve what God's will is—his good, pleasing, and perfect will.

The Father is saying, "You can expect resistance when you minister the word of God or serve where I have placed you" My grace is sufficient for you; ask for more for your assignments. Seek the Holy Spirit to reveal where I have called and appointed you, as being in My will is crucial.

Have faith in Me, and I will help you when hope seems distant. Come to the secret place and allow Me to overflow your cup. I desire to fill you from head to toe. When you face resistance, command the spirit of hindrance and retaliation to be cast back into the abyss in the name of Jesus. I am calling you to have a deeper relationship with me. Do not be surprised by the painful trials you encounter, as though something strange were happening.

SEPTEMBER 23ʳᵈ

Anointed Through the Warfare

Zephaniah 3:9

"Then I will purify the lips of the peoples, that all of them may call on the name of the Lord and serve him shoulder to shoulder.

Isaiah 58:12

Your people will rebuild the ancient ruins and will raise up the age-old foundations; you will be called Repairer of Broken Walls Restorer of Streets with Dwellings.

The Father is saying, "You have endured much warfare, pain, and crushing, but I have anointed you for these attacks and pressures." You were never alone, and I will never leave or forsake you. It's okay if not everyone likes or accepts you; remember, they first rejected Me.

I love you and am so proud of you. I am with you when others talk about you, misuse, or manipulate you. I see and hear everything; while people focus on appearances, I look at the heart. I see your pure and good heart.

I see you and am preparing a turnaround in your body, finances, and life. A turnaround is coming in Jesus' name. If you receive this, say Amen and thank you, Jesus.

SEPTEMBER 24TH

Strength Through the Spirit

Zechariah 4:1

Then, the angel who talked with me returned and woke me up like someone awakened from sleep.

The Father is saying, "Not by might nor by power, but by my Spirit," can we achieve all things. Through Christ, who empowers us, we find our strength. As you navigate today and seek to follow the will of our Father, remember it is only by the Spirit of the living God that you can endure and thrive.

Reflect on how you have overcome challenges in the past—perhaps earning a degree, acquiring a new car, or simply making it through a difficult year. These accomplishments are not solely due to your efforts but are testaments to the power of God working in your life.

SEPTEMBER 25TH

Trust and Re-focus

Isaiah 53:10

Yet it was the Lord's will to crush him and cause him to suffer, and though the Lord makes his life an offering for sin, he will see his offspring and prolong his days, and the will of the Lord will prosper in his hand.

Exodus 27:20

"Command the Israelites to bring you clear oil of pressed olives for the light so that the lamps may be kept burning.

The Father is saying, "Trust and believe in Me with all your heart, mind, and soul. Focus your full attention on Me." It's time to re-direct all your attention to Me. I am pouring My Spirit upon you. As the living water, I will fill you to overflow, and you will never thirst again.

I know you've been wondering about the turmoil in your life. I am breaking and crushing you because everything not of Me must be burned away. Your inner struggle and the dying of your flesh are part of the process. You asked to be refined, which is how new oil is produced.

Walk into your full potential, which will only happen through this process of being crushed.

SEPTEMBER 26TH

You Are My Battle-Ax

Jeremiah 1:9-10

Then the Lord reached out his hand and touched my mouth and said to me, "I have put my words in your mouth. ¹⁰ See, today I appoint you over nations and kingdoms to uproot and tear down, to destroy and overthrow, to build and to plant."

The Father is saying, "You are My battle, ax, and sword. Through you, I will shatter nations and destroy kingdoms. I will defeat armies, including their horses, riders, chariots, and charioteers. You are a force to be reckoned with, and the enemy is already defeated. I am in the process of reconciling everything that has been taken."

Do not be discouraged by what you see. The visible is temporary, but what you have in Me is eternal and filled with My glory. You carry My presence, and I am with you in every place and circumstance. Fear not the faces you encounter, for I am with you to deliver you.

Just as I touched Jeremiah's mouth, I am touching yours. I have placed My words in your mouth, My beloved."

SEPTEMBER 27TH

The Spirit of Excellence in Every Task

Nehemiah 4:17

Those who carried materials did their work with one hand and held a weapon in the other,

The Father is saying, "Consider the builders of the wall who worked with one hand supporting their load and the other holding a weapon. In the same way, ask My Holy Spirit for grace to endure the battles and hardships you face today. Seek wisdom to work at everything you do diligently, striving for excellence in all things.

Pray for the spirit of excellence to be upon you, enabling you to work hard and become proficient in your tasks for My glory. Let My glory shine through you and within you. You are equipped to be strong and courageous in all you undertake, for I have commanded you to be so beloved."

SEPTEMBER 28TH

Moving Forward with Faith

> Genesis 19:2

"My Lords," he said, "please turn aside to your servant's house. You can wash your feet and spend the night and then go on your way early in the morning."

"No," they answered, "we will spend the night in the square."

The Father is saying that you should consider how Lot and his family were urged to leave Sodom before its destruction. Lot's attachment to the city made his departure difficult, even as the messengers warned them. Similarly, some of you have become too comfortable where you are. I am calling you to step out in faith and trust that I am with you.

I have asked you to share the gospel, pray for the lost, and bring those wandering back home. Extend the grace to others that I have given to you. Do not look back or beside you; I control your life. Allow Me to guide you without hesitation. Trust in My direction and leave behind what I have already delivered you.

SEPTEMBER 29TH

A Covenant of Light

> 2 Corinthians 6:14

Do not be yoked together with unbelievers. For what do righteousness and wickedness have in common? Or what fellowship can light have with darkness?

The Father is saying, "Do not be unequally yoked with unbelievers. Righteousness and lawlessness have no partnership, and light does not fellowship with darkness." Beloved, you are in a covenant with Me, and I am in you. It is wise to maintain distance from those who deny Christ or the power of God.

Pray for them and share the good news of Jesus' love, but move on if they do not receive you. They are rejecting Me, not you. Seek guidance from My Holy Spirit and remember that you are now alive in Christ, having been transformed from your former ways. Continue to walk with Me, and together, we will accomplish great things for the kingdom of God.

SEPTEMBER 30ᵀᴴ

Trust in Silence

Revelation 22:13

I am the Alpha and the Omega, the First and the Last, the Beginning and the End.

Psalm 37:6

He will make your righteous reward shine like the dawn, your vindication like the noonday sun.

The Father is saying, "In this season, you need only to be silent. Refrain from defending yourself or proving anything; keep your mouth closed." I am your protector, defender, keeper, and friend. I will vindicate you publicly, and justice will prevail. I have seen how some mistreated you, and I know every injustice. Allow Me to be your advocate and work on your behalf. Stay where I can receive what I have for you and what I am about to do. Be still and know that I am God—Alpha and Omega, the beginning and the end."

OCTOBER 1ST

Embraced by Divine Love

Isaiah 61:7

Instead of your shame, you will receive a double portion,

and instead of disgrace, you will rejoice in your inheritance. And so you will inherit a double portion in your land, and everlasting joy will be yours.

1 John 1:9

If we confess our sins, he is faithful and just and will forgive us our sins and purify us from all unrighteousness.

The Father is saying, "I am yours, and you are mine. Nothing can separate you from my love." You are chosen and worthy to be my child because I am worthy. I am always with you—beside you and all around you. Even in your brokenness, you are still blessed. Surrender your marriage, plans, and desires to me. I wish to bless you and your children. Entrust me with all of you, including those parts you wish to keep hidden. I see, know, and still love you without condemnation or shame. All condemnation comes from the enemy. In me, there is only love. As the world's savior, I can heal every disease and deliver you from addiction. Be set free! Sit at my feet and minister to me. You are deeply loved."

OCTOBER 2ND

Empowered Through Christ

> Philippians 4:13

I can do all this through him, who gives me strength.

> Matthew 21:21

Jesus replied, "Truly I tell you, if you have faith and do not doubt, not only can you do what was done to the fig tree, but also you can say to this mountain, 'Go, throw yourself into the sea,' and it will be done.

The Father is saying, "You can do all things through Christ Jesus, who gives you strength." No giant will overcome you, and no mountain will remain unmoved. You have the power and authority to command that mountain to move in Jesus' name, and it will. Have faith and ask the Holy Spirit to align your thoughts with my Word, and it will be so. The enemy may try to discourage you and make you doubt my plans for your life, but remember that Satan is the father of lies. I am your true Father and will never leave or forsake you. When doubt burdens you, come to me and release all unbelief. Reject every lie of the enemy and trust in me, for I will never fail you. The Most High God loves you.

OCTOBER 3ᴿᴰ

Unshakeable Strength in Christ

1 John 1:9

If we confess our sins, he is faithful and just and will forgive us our sins and purify us from all unrighteousness.

1 Peter 5:6-7

Humble yourselves, therefore, under God's mighty hand, that he may lift you up in due time. ⁷ Cast all your anxiety on him because he cares for you.

The Father is saying, "Humble yourself under my mighty hand, and in due time, I will lift you up. I know the burdens you carry, and I care for you deeply. Cast all your worries, fears, and anxieties on me, for I am with you and will give you peace. The enemy may try to fill your heart with fear and doubt, but remember, I am faithful. Trust in my love for you; know I will never leave or let you down. You are never alone because I care for and will always be beside you."

OCTOBER 4ᵀᴴ

Standing Firm in Divine Strength

Isaiah 54:17

no weapon forged against you will prevail, and you will refute every tongue that accuses you. This is the heritage of the servants of the Lord, and this is their vindication from me," declares the Lord.

Romans 12:2

Do not conform to the pattern of this world, but be transformed by the renewing of your mind. Then, you will be able to test and approve what God's will is—his good, pleasing, and perfect will.

The Father is saying, "When the enemy comes to steal, kill, and destroy, remain faithful and obedient, for the weapon may form, but it will never prosper." Trials will come and go, but stand firm against every attack. Rebuke every plot, plan, and scheme in the name of Jesus. My name is above every other name. Everything you need has been placed inside you. Fight back, and don't back down. The enemy may try to intimidate you but reject the spirit of fear in Jesus' name. In my name, every enemy, mountain, and storm must flee. Ask the Holy Spirit to renew your mind and put on the full armor of God. There is no giant too big for the Lord!

OCTOBER 5ᵀᴴ

Feeding Your Spirit with Faith

> 1 Peter 5:8

Be alert and of sober mind. Your enemy, the devil, prowls around like a roaring lion, looking for someone to devour.

The Father is saying, "Faith comes by hearing my Word." Be mindful of what you feed your spirit and careful about what you watch. The enemy prowls around like a lion, seeking whom he may devour. Notice that it says, 'like a lion'—the enemy may think he is powerful, but he is nothing compared to me. Be alert and focus on feeding your spirit with my Word. Come to me with expectancy and child-like faith, ready to receive all I can offer. I have been waiting for you. Take each day as it comes and lay down every burden, worry, and stress at my feet. I will give you a peace that surpasses all understanding. Amidst many distractions, remember that I, your Father and King, determine what is truly important. Rebuke all distractions in Jesus' name. I will be with you, even when you walk on water.

OCTOBER 6ᵀᴴ

2 Corinthians 5:7

For we live by faith, not by sight.

James 1:6

But when you ask, you must believe and not doubt because the one who doubts is like a wave of the sea, blown and tossed by the wind.

The Father is saying, "Walk by faith and not by sight." While you may sometimes be swayed by your emotions, do not let feelings lead you; instead, be guided by the Spirit of the living God. The Holy Spirit will direct and guide you. Remember, emotions are temporary, but my Spirit is eternal. Ask the Holy Spirit to strengthen your faith as you seek my will. This journey with me requires trust. Listen to my still, small voice guiding you in the right direction. I will never lead you astray. When you feel my Spirit calling you to be obedient and follow my direction, remember that I am your shepherd, and you are my sheep. One of the enemy's tactics is doubt—resist it. Have faith in me, and I will lead you through any valley. There is no mountain or giant too big for me. Whatever you face, you do not face it alone.

OCTOBER 7ᵀᴴ

Letting Go and Trusting in His Grace

2 Corinthians 12:9

But he said to me, "My grace is sufficient for you, for my power is made perfect in weakness." Therefore, I will boast all the more gladly about my weaknesses so that Christ's power may rest on me.

Psalms 139:7-8

Where can I go from your Spirit? Where can I flee from your presence? [8] If I go up to the heavens, you are there; if I make my bed in the depths, you are there.

The Father is saying, "Release all your burdens to me today. Those burdens were never meant for you." When you let go of every worry and fear, the hindrance blocking your ability to hear me will be lifted. I am fighting every battle, big and small. I love you, my beloved, and all that you care about. When the enemy attacks, call on my name—I am always with you. My presence surrounds you, so you are never alone. If you need grace today, whether for your home, your children, your marriage, or any relationship, ask me, and you will receive it. My grace is sufficient, and you will lack nothing."

OCTOBER 8ᵀᴴ

Overcoming Fear with Divine Strength

John 15:18-25

"If the world hates you, keep in mind that it hated me first. ¹⁹ If you belonged to the world, it would love you as its own. As it is, you do not belong to the world, but I have chosen you out of the world. That is why the world hates you. ²⁰ Remember what I told you: 'A servant is not greater than his master.' If they persecuted me, they will persecute you also. If they obeyed my teaching, they will obey yours also. ²¹ They will treat you this way because of my name, for they do not know the one who sent me.²² If I had not come and spoken to them, they would not be guilty of sin, but now they have no excuse for their sin. ²³ Whoever hates me hates my Father as well. ²⁴ If I had not done among them the works no one else did, they would not be guilty of sin. As it is, they have seen, and yet they have hated both me and my Father. ²⁵ But this is to fulfill what is written in their Law: 'They hated me without reason.'

2 Chronicles 20:15

He said: "Listen, King Jehoshaphat and all who live in Judah and Jerusalem! This is what the Lord says: 'Do not be afraid or discouraged because of this vast army. For the battle is not yours, but God's.

The Father is saying, "Do not let fear creep in. The enemy uses fear to hinder my children, but as a child of God, you lack nothing." When you feel anxiety or fear attacking you, rebuke those spirits in the name of Jesus. Declare, 'Jesus, I am strong; I know my God fights for me.' The Lord is your strong tower, and His rod and staff comfort you. You need not be afraid. Rejoice and remain glad even in suffering or when others reject you without cause—it is not you that they reject, but me first. Pray continually and give thanks in all circumstances. Come to worship and praise me for all I have done and what I am about to do. I love you, my beloved. The battle is not yours; it is mine. Fight the good fight of faith."

OCTOBER 9ᵀᴴ

Facing Challenges with Divine Support

> Deuteronomy 8:18

But remember the Lord your God, for it is he who gives you the ability to produce wealth and so confirms his covenant, which he swore to your ancestors, as it is today.

The Father is saying, "No matter what you face, I face it with you." You can confront every enemy tactic with, 'I rebuke you, Satan,' and he will flee in my name. I know this journey hasn't been easy, but I never promised ease—only that you can do everything through Christ, who strengthens you. I will extend my grace to help you achieve your goals, and remember; I give you the power to gain wealth and confirm the covenant I made with your forefathers. I empower you to be successful. If you are uncertain about your efforts, ask the Holy Spirit for reassurance that I am always with you."

OCTOBER 10TH

Embracing Divine Power and Perfection

Luke 10:19

I have given you authority to trample on snakes and scorpions and to overcome all the power of the enemy; nothing will harm you.

John 10:10

The thief comes only to steal and kill and destroy; I have come that they may have life and have it to the full.

Hebrews 12:2

fixing our eyes on Jesus, the pioneer and perfecter of faith. For the joy set before him, he endured the cross, scorning its shame, and sat down at the right hand of the throne of God.

The Father is saying, "Refuse to doubt and fear!" When the enemy tries to steal, kill, and destroy, remember that I have given you power and authority over all the enemy's schemes. Nothing will harm you. I know you wonder if you are doing enough for me. My beloved, you are perfect as you are. Just love me with all your heart, mind, and soul, and obey my will. You don't need to strive for perfection; I am the perfecter and author of your faith. Trust me and follow my guidance. I see and hear everything. I am the King of kings and Lord of Lords, and you are perfect for me.

OCTOBER 11ᵀᴴ

Seeking God Over People

Hebrews 11:6

And without faith, it is impossible to please God, because anyone who comes to him must believe that he exists and that he rewards those who earnestly seek him.

Galatians 1:10

Am I now trying to win the approval of human beings or of God? Or am I trying to please people? If I were still trying to please people, I would not be a servant of Christ.

The Father is saying, "Avoid being a people pleaser and focus on pleasing me instead." Seeking to please others can lead to idolatry. Repent and turn back to me; I am here with open arms. I know you are tired and feel overwhelmed, but you have the strength to continue. The enemy is a deceiver who attacks when you are vulnerable. Find rest in me and seek me with all your heart. I will always be with you. Dedicate time to commune with me, for without faith, it is impossible to please me. You must believe that I am and that I reward those who diligently seek me and fight the good fight of faith."

OCTOBER 12ᵀᴴ

Finding Rest in His Promise

Matthew 11:28-30

"Come to me, all you who are weary and burdened, and I will give you rest. ²⁹ Take my yoke upon you and learn from me, for I am gentle and humble in heart, and you will find rest for your souls. ³⁰ For my yoke is easy, and my burden is light."

Romans 15:13

May the God of hope fill you with all joy and peace as you trust in him so that you may overflow with hope by the power of the Holy Spirit.

The Father is saying, "Come to me, all who are weary and burdened, and I will give you rest." Take my yoke upon you and learn from me, for I am gentle and humble, and you will find rest for your souls. My yoke is easy, and my burden is light. I know it's difficult not to see what I'm doing behind the scenes. Even when nothing seems to be moving, continue to press forward. Hold on a bit longer; I am working everything out for your good. Trust in me! What I have in store for you is the best, and I will never give my children mere crumbs. Your faith in me will lead you to the next level. Get ready, get set, go! You can do this, and I will be with you."

OCTOBER 13TH

A Table Prepared in the Wilderness

Psalm 20:6

Now this I know: The Lord gives victory to his anointed. He answers him from his heavenly sanctuary with the victorious power of his right hand.

Isaiah 59:19

From the west, people will fear the name of the Lord, and from the rising of the sun, they will revere his glory. For he will come like a pent-up flood that the breath of the Lord drives along.

The Father is saying, "As I lead you out of the wilderness, I have prepared a table in the presence of your enemies." I anoint your head with oil and your cup overflows. Don't be swayed by what you see even when I'm not moving in your life. Have faith and believe I am constantly at work in every area of your life. Satan is a liar; I am always moving, rearranging things and people to bring order back into your life. Call on my name, Jesus—I am always near when you feel distant. Rest in my presence, knowing you are my child, and I am your Father. Your future is secured in me. Although you've faced many trials and focused on the attacks, fix your eyes on me and worship through every battle, for the victory has already been won. I grant victory to my anointed. When the enemy comes in like a flood, the Spirit of the Lord will raise a standard against him."

OCTOBER 14TH

Embracing the Promises of God

Isaiah 41:9-10

I took you from the ends of the earth, from its farthest corners, I called you. I said, 'You are my servant'; I have chosen you and have not rejected you. ¹⁰ So do not fear, for I am with you; do not be dismayed, for I am your God. I will strengthen you and help you; I will uphold you with my righteous right hand.

Psalm 91:11-12

For he will command his angels concerning you to guard you in all your ways; ¹² they will lift you up in their hands, so that you will not strike your foot against a stone.

The Father is saying, "Do not doubt what I have already spoken to you; what I have promised will come to pass. Celebrate every victory we have already won, beloved. I have so much I want to share with you and even more in store. The blessings I have for you are beyond measure. Everything you need is already within you. I have chosen and not rejected you, so do not fear, for I am with you; do not be dismayed, for I am your God. I will strengthen and help you, upholding you with my righteous right hand. I have commissioned angels to protect you from the evil one. Pray over your home, your family, and all that concerns you. Plead the blood of Jesus over yourself in my name. Demons will flee at the mention of my name. I will continually guide and lead you into all truth."

OCTOBER 15ᵗʰ

Facing Each Day with Divine Presence

Psalm 23:4

Even though I walk through the darkest valley, I will fear no evil, for you are with me; your rod and your staff, they comfort me.

Isaiah 45:5

I am the Lord, and there is no other; apart from me, there is no God.

I will strengthen you, though you have not acknowledged me,

The Father is saying, "Take one day and one step at a time. I am always with you. Some of my children forget that I know what you are facing." You are never alone in any trial, battle, or storm. I am your Lord and Savior, three in one. Amidst many distractions and voices, remember that only one thing matters: your relationship with me. I need your full attention. Though you walk through the valley of the shadow of death, you will fear no evil, for I am with you; my rod and staff comfort you. No matter what you face today, we will face it together. Put on the whole armor of God, for I will protect you, my beloved.

OCTOBER 16TH

Triumph Through the Process

Matthew 4:4

Jesus answered, "It is written: 'Man shall not live on bread alone, but on every word that comes from the mouth of God.

Acts 3:20-21

and that he may send the Messiah, who has been appointed for you—even Jesus. ²¹ Heaven must receive him until the time comes for God to restore everything, as he promised long ago through his holy prophets.

The Father is saying, "You have passed the tests!" You stood firm despite the pressure from attacks and the enemy's attempts to use circumstances, people, and distractions to derail you. Each time the enemy struck, you rose and fought back. The process you're enduring is necessary; it builds your character and strengthens your faith. When you feel empty, come to me and let my presence fill you. I desire to offer you living water so you will never thirst again. Remember, man cannot live on bread alone but on every word that comes from the mouth of God. Ask the Holy Spirit to renew your mind and rejuvenate your soul. Though you are tired, I am restoring and reviving you to bring you back into order.

OCTOBER 17ᵀᴴ

Breaking Free from the Enemy's Trap

James 4:2

You desire but do not have, so you kill. You covet, but you cannot get what you want, so you quarrel and fight. You do not have because you do not ask God.

Ephesians 4:27

and do not give the devil a foothold.

The Father is saying, "Do not fall into the enemy's trap." Many of my children cling to unforgiveness, anger, and bitterness, providing only a foothold for the enemy. Letting go of these things will free you from the enemy's bondages and remove any foothold for his schemes. Choose joy and peace today; I give them to you freely. You have not because you ask not. When you ask in my name with faith, it will be given to you. You will grow stronger and wiser as you come out of the wilderness. When the enemy reminds you of your past, remind him of his future. Release any unforgiveness or other burdens the Holy Spirit leads you to, and receive your freedom today in Jesus' name.

OCTOBER 18ᵀᴴ

Rejoicing Amidst the Enemy's Attacks

Philippians 4:6

Do not be anxious about anything, but in every situation, by prayer and petition, with thanksgiving, present your requests to God.

John 15:5

"I am the vine; you are the branches. If you remain in me and I in you, you will bear much fruit; apart from me, you can do nothing.

The Father is saying, "You are a target for the enemy, but rejoice, for I have chosen you and not rejected you. I have called you by name and set you apart for this time." The attacks you face are evidence of your significance in the spiritual realm. You are a threat to the kingdom of darkness. As you go through this day, focus on me rather than the attacks, which are merely distractions. Pray continually and stay in communion with me; Satan will flee because you possess the power and authority that comes from me dwelling within you. Use the authority I've given you, for the anointing of your life is a blessing. Be still and know that I am God. Ask the Holy Spirit for grace to navigate today's challenges. My grace is sufficient, and you are bearing much fruit in my name. The fruits of the Spirit—love, joy, peace, patience, kindness, goodness, gentleness, faithfulness, and self-control—will be evident in you. Bring all your concerns to me in prayer.

OCTOBER 19ᵀᴴ

Faithfulness in the Midst of Pressure

> Matthew 7:15-20

"Watch out for false prophets. They come to you in sheep's clothing, but inwardly, they are ferocious wolves. ¹⁶ By their fruit, you will recognize them. Do people pick grapes from thornbushes, or figs from thistles? ¹⁷ Likewise, every good tree bears good fruit, but a bad tree bears bad fruit. ¹⁸ A good tree cannot bear bad fruit, and a bad tree cannot bear good fruit.¹⁹ Every tree that does not bear good fruit is cut down and thrown into the fire. ²⁰ Thus, by their fruit, you will recognize them.

The Father is saying, "Remain faithful even as you feel the pressure." Know that you are standing strong! Your eyes and ears are open; you now see people, places, and things through my perspective. Continue to seek me, for I am giving you glory in Jesus' name. Behold, I am doing something new—do you not perceive it? I am making a way in the wilderness and streams in the wasteland. Be mindful of those you allow into your life, and ask the Holy Spirit to reveal the true nature of the people around you. Some are sent by me, and others by the evil one. Ask the Holy Spirit to increase your spiritual discernment. You have not because you ask not. Remember, Satan is the father of lies and disguises evil as good. Beware of false prophets who use my name but lack true power. I am the source of all power and authority; you will recognize them by their fruits.

OCTOBER 20ᵀᴴ

Trusting God's Perfect Plan

Nehemiah 8:10

Nehemiah said, "Go and enjoy choice food and sweet drinks, and send some to those who have nothing prepared. This day is holy to our Lord. Do not grieve, for the joy of the Lord is your strength."

Isaiah 58:6

"Is not this the kind of fasting I have chosen: to loose the chains of injustice and untie the cords of the yoke, to set the oppressed free and break every yoke?

Jeremiah 29:11

For I know the plans I have for you," declares the Lord, "plans to prosper you and not to harm you, plans to give you hope and a future.

The Father is saying, "Do not doubt what I have planned for you." What I have spoken will come to pass in Jesus' name. Refuse to worry about the future. Have I not said, 'For I know the plans I have for you, declares the Lord, plans to prosper you and not to harm you, plans to give you hope and a future? I am the Lord your God and control every situation and circumstance. Will you trust me? I have never failed or let you down, and I know what is best for you. Release every burden to me, including those concerning your family. I am the savior of the world. Do not carry false burdens that are not yours to carry, as they can open the door to a spirit of heaviness. I died on the cross for your brokenness and anxiety, and I rose again on the third day. The enemy seeks to rob you of your joy and peace. Let your guard down so I can work freely in your life.

OCTOBER 21ST

Embracing God's Unconditional Love

Romans 8:1

Therefore, there is now no condemnation for those who are in Christ Jesus,

Luke 22:31

"Simon, Simon, Satan has asked to sift all of you as wheat.

The Father is saying, "You have been striving, but there is no need to strive, beloved. You don't have to earn my love; I freely give it to you when you ask."

I am here with open arms, always welcoming you into my presence. It's not a feeling you seek but my presence. I am in you, and my Spirit dwells within you, guiding and teaching you. If your mind drifts due to a lack of trust, surrender your shame and self-condemnation today. There is no condemnation for those who are in Christ Jesus. When the enemy tempts you with lies, remind him of who you are in me and that you walk daily with me, surrendering to my will.

OCTOBER 22ND

Comfort in Every Trial

1 Corinthians 10:13

No temptation has overtaken you except what is common to mankind. And God is faithful; he will not let you be tempted beyond what you can bear. But when you are tempted, he will also provide a way out so that you can endure it.

Psalm 23:1-6

The Lord is my shepherd; I lack nothing. ²He makes me lie down in green pastures; he leads me beside quiet waters,³ he refreshes my soul. He guides me along the right paths for his name's sake. ⁴ Even though I walk through the darkest valley, I will fear no evil, for you are with me; your rod and your staff, they comfort me.

The Father is saying, "You will face trials and tribulations, but remember, you will never face anything alone. Even though you walk through the valley of the shadow of death, you will fear no evil, for I am with you; my rod and staff comfort you. I am with you through every trial and circumstance. Take hold of my hand and trust in me; listen for my still, small voice calling from within. I will never lead you astray. Despite daily challenges, you are never alone. Ask my Holy Spirit to fill you with my presence so your mind aligns with the Word of God. The enemy may tempt you, but he must ask me for permission. I will never allow you to be tempted beyond what you can bear, my beloved."

OCTOBER 23ʳᵈ

Precious and Complete in Me

Proverbs 3:15

She is more precious than rubies; nothing you desire can compare with her.

Psalm 23:5

You prepare a table before me in the presence of my enemies. You anoint my head with oil; my cup overflows.

The Father is saying, "You are more precious than rubies." If you need to do more or feel inadequate, remember you are already everything I've called you to be. Everything you need is within you—it is me. You lack nothing, and you are enough. You are beautiful, created in my image. Come and commune with me; soak in my presence. Let me refresh you and anoint you with my oil. You are worthy, beautiful, handsome, intelligent, and royal. You are clothed in righteousness. I know your name. Anything you ask in my name, I will give to you.

OCTOBER 24th

Righteousness in Humility

Exodus 3:6

Then he said, "I am the God of your father,[a] the God of Abraham, the God of Isaac, and the God of Jacob." At this, Moses hid his face because he was afraid to look at God.

Matthew 6:34

Therefore, do not worry about tomorrow, for tomorrow will worry about itself. Each day has enough trouble of its own.

The Father is saying, "Be mindful not to practice righteousness for the sake of others." Remember, it is through me that you are made holy and whole. Begin each day with thanksgiving, for I am the great I Am. Humble yourself daily and recognize that I am God. I can move mountains from here to there. I created you and see every part of you. Do not worry about tomorrow; it has enough trouble of its own. Everything you need is already within you. For any decision, come to me and ask rather than seek others' advice. If you lack anything, come to me, and I will give it freely. I am the God of Abraham, Isaac, and Jacob. You have victory in every situation, circumstance, or battle through the Lamb's blood and the power of your testimony.

OCTOBER 25TH

Trusting in God's Provision

Hebrews 4:9-11

There remains, then, a Sabbath-rest for the people of God;[10] for anyone who enters God's rest also rests from their works, just as God did from his. [11] Let us, therefore, make every effort to enter that rest, so that no one will perish by following their example of disobedience.

Isaiah 40:31

but those who hope in the Lord will renew their strength. They will soar on wings like eagles; they will run and not grow weary; they will walk and not be faint.

The Father is saying, "You will lack no good thing. Whatever you ask in my name, you shall receive. Even if you are feeling under the weather, let the Holy Spirit guide you rather than your feelings. I am with you whether you call from the East or the West. If you sense something trying to attach itself to you through an enemy attack, rebuke that evil spirit and ask the Holy Spirit to reveal what is hidden. When you are tired, seek the Holy Spirit's guidance on whether to rest or continue praying. Rest in my presence, and I will renew your strength. Allow my love to fill your heart and mind."

OCTOBER 26ᵀᴴ

Overcoming Fear with God's Presence

2 Timothy 1:7

For the Spirit God gave us does not make us timid but gives us power, love, and self-discipline.

Isaiah 41:9-10

I took you from the ends of the earth, from its farthest corners, called you. I said, 'You are my servant'; I have chosen you and have not rejected you. ¹⁰ So do not fear, for I am with you; do not be dismayed, for I am your God. I will strengthen you and help you; I will uphold you with my righteous right hand.

The Father is saying, "Do not let fear cripple you." Many of my children worry about the future or the present, but fear is unnecessary. This is one of Satan's greatest tactics—tricking you into believing that you are powerless. Rebuke every demonic attack and command Satan to leave in the name of Jesus. Remember, God has not given us a spirit of fear but one of power, love, and self-discipline. When you feel afraid, call on my name, and I will be with you, helping you walk through challenges. Ask the Holy Spirit to take you deeper with me. I have chosen you and will not reject you. Do not fear, for I am with you. I will strengthen and help you, upholding you with my righteous right hand.

OCTOBER 27ᵀᴴ

Trusting God's Provision

Revelation 3:7-8

"To the angel of the church in Philadelphia, write:

These are the words of him who is holy and true, who holds the key of David. What he opens, no one can shut, and what he shuts, no one can open. ⁸ I know your deeds. See, I have placed before you an open door that no one can shut. I know that you have little strength, yet you have kept my word and have not denied my name.

Philippians 4:6-7

Do not be anxious about anything, but in every situation, by prayer and petition, with thanksgiving, present your requests to God. ⁷ And the peace of God, which transcends all understanding, will guard your hearts and your minds in Christ Jesus.

The Father is saying, "No man or enemy can close the doors I open. I am the one who opens the floodgates of heaven and blesses you. I will supply all your needs. Trust in me, not the world, for it is temporary, while my word and life are eternal. When you feel overwhelmed, pray and ask me to drive out every unclean spirit and lie in my name. Take every thought captive and make it obedient to Christ Jesus. I am with you, and you shall receive anything you ask in my name. Remember, faith is essential in all you do."

OCTOBER 28TH

Embracing God's Presence

> Deuteronomy 31:6

Be strong and courageous. Do not be afraid or terrified because of them, for the Lord your God goes with you; he will never leave you nor forsake you."

> 1 John 2:27

As for you, the anointing you received from him remains in you, and you do not need anyone to teach you. But as his anointing teaches you about all things and as that anointing is real, not counterfeit—just as it has taught you, remain in him.

The Father is saying, "You often wonder about life without the sacrifice of my Son on the cross. Remember, I love you deeply and have chosen and anointed you for this time. Every promise I've made to you will come to pass. I see your heart and the love you have for others. I hear your bold prayers and see your pain. It's okay to cry when you hurt—come to me and pour out everything. I know you intimately, even the number of hairs on your head. Let my presence fill you and reveal my plans. You are never alone; I will never leave or forsake you."

OCTOBER 29TH

Embracing Your New Identity

Hebrews 13:8

Jesus Christ is the same yesterday and today and forever.

1 Corinthians 6:20

you were bought at a price. Therefore, honor God with your bodies.

The Father is saying, "Don't let the worries of this world burden you." You are set apart as holy to me, chosen from all nations as my special treasure. The old you is gone; you are a new creation in Christ Jesus. Ask my Holy Spirit to shift your perspective, to see people, places, and circumstances as I do. Don't let fleeting emotions dictate your identity. You were bought with a price—the sacrifice of my Son. I am unchanging, the same yesterday, today, and forever. Trust in who I've made you to be.

OCTOBER 30ᵀᴴ

Rediscovering What Was Lost

Isaiah 43:19

See, I am doing a new thing! Now it springs up; do you not perceive it? I am making a way in the wilderness and streams in the wasteland.

Philippians 4:19

And my God will meet all your needs according to the riches of his glory in Christ Jesus.

The Father is saying, "What you thought you lost is now being found." I am doing a new thing; can you perceive it? I am making a way in the wilderness and streams in the wasteland. What you felt was lost—people, things, desires—I am bringing new blessings into your life. I have placed those desires in your heart and am making a way for them to come to fruition. I will never leave or forsake you, for you are the apple of my eye. Trust that I will supply all your needs.

OCTOBER 31ST

Standing Firm in Faith

> 1 Corinthians 10:20-21

No, but the sacrifices of pagans are offered to demons, not to God, and I do not want you to be participants with demons. [21] You cannot drink the cup of the Lord and the cup of demons, too; you cannot have a part in both the Lord's table and the table of demons.

> Ephesians 5:11'

Have nothing to do with the fruitless deeds of darkness but rather expose them.

The Father is saying, "Do not compromise on this day." While Halloween may seem innocent, there is much darkness behind this holiday. Witches and warlocks engage in witchcraft and spells. Even if you want to take your children trick-or-treating, resist the temptation to participate. Instead, glorify My holy name through praise and prayer. Celebrate the greatest gift I have given you—My Son, Jesus Christ. Remember, 'For God so loved the world that He gave His only Son, that whoever believes in Him shall not perish but have eternal life.' Bring light into the darkness and seek My guidance through the Holy Spirit. Avoid opening doors to witchcraft and give no foothold to the enemy. Your best interest is always My priority, and I love you dearly."

NOVEMBER 1ˢᵀ

Embracing Freedom Through Christ

Proverbs 14:30-35

A heart at peace gives life to the body, but envy rots the bones. ³¹Whoever oppresses the poor shows contempt for their Maker, but whoever is kind to the needy honors God. ³² When calamity comes, the wicked are brought down, but even in death, the righteous seek refuge in God. ³³ Wisdom reposes in the heart of the discerning, and even among fools, she lets herself be known.³⁴ Righteousness exalts a nation, but sin condemns any people. ³⁵ A king delights in a wise servant, but a shameful servant arouses his fury

Luke 6:27

"But to you who are listening, I say: Love your enemies, do good to those who hate you,

The Father is saying, "With Me, you can do everything through Christ who strengthens you. There is no limit to what I can accomplish in your life." Do not settle for less than the fullness of what I offer. As a beloved child of the one true King, you will be granted anything you ask in Jesus' name. All it takes is a mustard seed of faith.

If there is any unforgiveness in your heart—toward a friend, family member, or anyone—be quick to release and forgive. Remember, they may not fully understand the impact of their actions. Unforgiveness can spread like a harmful disease within you. It is far better to forgive and let go. Pray for your enemies and show kindness to those who may harbor ill will towards you.

Though you are in this world, you are not of it. Bring any pain or trauma to Me and release it, for it was never meant to be your burden. Allow yourself to be free from these weights today, in Jesus' name.

NOVEMBER 2ND

Trusting the Waymaker

1 Corinthians 2:9

However, as it is written: "What no eye has seen, what no ear has heard,

and what no human mind has conceived"—

the things God has prepared for those who love him—

Isaiah 64:4

Since ancient times no one has heard,

no ear has perceived,

no eye has seen any God besides you,

who acts on behalf of those who wait for him.

The Father is saying, "Refuse to doubt what I can do in your life." I am the Waymaker, the Lord, your Holy One, the Creator of Israel, your King. I make a way through the sea and a path through the mighty waters. As the Apostle Paul wrote, "What no eye has seen, nor ear heard, nor the heart of man imagined, God has prepared for those who love Him.

Your human mind cannot fully grasp what I have in store for you. When you removed the limits you had placed on Me, your life began to change. I am a big God, a supernatural God. When I open a door for you, no one can close it. Seek My Holy Spirit to reveal these things to you. If you lack wisdom, ask, and I will give it generously.

NOVEMBER 3ᴿᴰ

Finding Peace in My Presence

2 Corinthians 5:17

Therefore, if anyone is in Christ, the new creation has come:[a] The old has gone, the new is here!

Colossians 3:15-17

Let the peace of Christ rule in your hearts since, as members of one body, you were called to peace. And be thankful. ¹⁶ Let the message of Christ dwell among you richly as you teach and admonish one another with all wisdom through psalms, hymns, and songs from the Spirit, singing to God with gratitude in your hearts. ¹⁷ And whatever you do, whether in word or deed, do it all in the name of the Lord Jesus, giving thanks to God the Father through him.

The Father is saying, "All is well, my beloved. There is no need to rush through life." Take time to immerse yourself in My presence. Let Me fill you, from the crown of your head to the soles of your feet. I desire to touch every dry place in your life, including those you may not know. Invite My Holy Spirit to fill every part of your being.

Embrace the process of transformation and renewal each day. I am replacing the old with the new within you. As Scripture promises, "If anyone is in Christ, the new creation has come; the old has gone, and a new life has begun." Rejoice and be glad. Thank Me in every circumstance and battle, and practice thanksgiving in all you do. Do not give the enemy any room in your life.

NOVEMBER 4ᵀᴴ

Remaining Steadfast in My Love

Luke 7:38

As she stood behind him at his feet weeping, she began to wet his feet with her tears. Then she wiped them with her hair, kissed them, and poured perfume on them.

Matthew 5:15

Neither do people light a lamp and put it under a bowl. Instead, they put it on its stand, and it gives light to everyone in the house.

The Father is saying that while others are preoccupied with the worries and concerns of this world, you remain steadfast. Like Mary Magdalene, you love Me deeply and follow My commandments. Amidst the distractions that captivate others, you offer your tears, wipe them with your hair, kiss, and anoint with precious ointment.

Worship and praise Me, for I have called you worthy, delivered you, and set you free from all bondage. I have set you apart as a light in this world. A city on a hill cannot be hidden. Do not hide your light; let it shine for all to see. Look at what I have done; all of this I have done for you.

NOVEMBER 5ᵀᴴ

Embracing Your Call and Trusting My Provision

Matthew 6:26-34

Look at the birds of the air; they do not sow or reap or store away in barns, and yet your heavenly Father feeds them. Are you not much more valuable than they? ²⁷ Can any one of you, by worrying, add a single hour to your life? ²⁸"And why do you worry about clothes? See how the flowers of the field grow. They do not labor or spin. ²⁹ Yet I tell you that not even Solomon in all his splendor was dressed like one of these.³⁰ If that is how God clothes the grass of the field, which is here today and tomorrow is thrown into the fire, will he not much more clothe you—you of little faith? ³¹ So do not worry, saying, 'What shall we eat?' or 'What shall we drink?' or 'What shall we wear?'³² For the pagans run after all these things, and your heavenly Father knows that you need them. ³³ But seek first his kingdom and his righteousness, and all these things will be given to you as well. ³⁴ Therefore, do not worry about tomorrow, for tomorrow will worry about itself. Each day has enough trouble of its own

Deuteronomy 28:12

The Lord will open the heavens, the storehouse of his bounty, to send rain on your land in season and to bless all the work of your hands. You will lend to many nations but will borrow from none.

The Father is saying that now is the time to share the good news. If you are called to preach, then preach; if to teach, then teach; if to serve, then serve. Seek My Holy Spirit to guide you. Ask the Holy Spirit to reveal your calling if you are unsure. Remember, you do not have to because you do not ask. Whatever you ask in My name, I will give you in Jesus' name.

I am the Lord who provides all your needs. Consider the birds of the air—they do not sow, reap, or store food, yet your Heavenly Father feeds them. You are far more valuable to Me than they are. I will bless your storehouses and every action of your hands. I will bless you in the land I am giving you. Trust in My provision and embrace My call on your life.

NOVEMBER 6ᵀᴴ

Standing Firm in My Truth

Joshua 3:5

Joshua told the people, "Consecrate yourselves, for tomorrow the Lord will do amazing things among you."

Solomon 2:10

My beloved spoke and said to me, "Arise, my darling, my beautiful one, come with me.

The Father is saying that when you doubt, confusion sets in, and the enemy will exploit that confusion. Do not doubt Me or the promises I have spoken over you. When you sense the enemy bringing confusion, seek My strategy. Stand firm against every plot, plan, and scheme, and be wise as a serpent yet innocent as a dove.

I reward those who seek Me with their hearts and immerse themselves in the Bread of the Word. Consecrate yourself to My Word alone; I am all you need. Avoid being consumed by the things of this world or putting Me last. I must always be first in your life. Remember, you are not of this world, my beloved. I love you and will always be with you.

NOVEMBER 7ᵀᴴ

Called to Holiness and Trust

Proverbs 3:5

Trust in the Lord with all your heart and lean not on your own understanding;

Philippians 4:19

And my God will meet all your needs according to the riches of his glory in Christ Jesus.

The Father is saying, "I am a holy God, and you are called to be holy." You are precious in My sight, and I am working daily in your life to provide the understanding you seek. Every word I have spoken will come to pass—either soon or has already been fulfilled. I am transforming you daily, removing what does not belong, and placing new desires and opportunities before you.

New opportunities are on the horizon. Depend on Me alone and trust Me with all your heart, soul, and mind. Do not rely on your understanding. If you need anything, ask in My name, in Jesus' name, and you will receive according to My will. Focus on what you have rather than what you lack. Thank Me for all I have given you. Remember, the enemy is the father of lies, but I am your God and will supply all your needs.

NOVEMBER 8TH

Rejoicing Through Trials

Isaiah 43:2

When you pass through the waters, I will be with you, and when you pass through the rivers, they will not sweep over you. When you walk through the fire, you will not be burned; the flames will not set you ablaze.

Deuteronomy 3:22

Do not be afraid of them; the Lord your God himself will fight for you."

The Father is saying that you will face hardships, persecution, and many trials, but rejoice and be glad, for you endure these for the sake of your Father. The battle is not yours; it is Mine, says the Lord. When you pass through the waters, I will be with you, and when you go through the rivers, they will not overwhelm you. Though you walk through the fire, the flames will not consume you.

I am for you; if I am for you, who can be against you? You may not yet see it physically, but a shift has already occurred, and that shift is in you. You are moving toward your destiny. Remember this, my beloved: I am always with you, no matter what you face. I am for you, and you need not fear, for the Lord your God fights for you.

NOVEMBER 9TH

Surrendering Completely to God

1 Peter 2-3

Ephesians 4:31-32

Get rid of all bitterness, rage and anger, brawling and slander, along with every form of malice. ³² Be kind and compassionate to one another, forgiving each other, just as in Christ God forgave you

Deuteronomy 26:9

He brought us to this place and gave us this land, a land flowing with milk and honey;

The Father is saying that you should surrender every aspect of your life to Me. Some of My children try to straddle the line between the world and My presence, but I desire all of you in My embrace. You are whole and complete in Me. You may wonder where I am, but I have never left; I have been waiting for you.

Let go of all malice, deceit, hypocrisy, envy, and slander. By doing so, you will grow in your salvation, having tasted that the Lord is good. Lay down today every regret, tarnish, doubt, and fear. These things are of the enemy and serve no purpose where I am leading you. I will fulfill everything in your life, guiding you to a place where milk and honey overflow.

NOVEMBER 10TH

Submitting to God and Finding True Freedom

James 4:7-8

Submit yourselves, then, to God. Resist the devil, and he will flee from you. ⁸ Come near to God, and he will come near to you. Wash your hands, you sinners, and purify your hearts, you double-minded.

1 Thessalonians 5:3

While people are saying "Peace and safety," destruction will come on them suddenly, as labor pains on a pregnant woman, and they will not escape.

The Father is saying to submit yourselves to Me. Resist the devil, and he will flee from you. When you align yourself with My authority and turn away from your wicked ways, resist the devil, and he will flee from you in Jesus' name. Walk by faith, not by sight.

Cleanse your hands and purify your hearts. You cannot serve both yourself and Me. Purify your heart and turn from all sin. Living for this world leads to destruction, but living for Me brings eternal life in heaven. My grace is sufficient for you, my beloved. It is time to end relationships and habits that no longer serve you. I have been nudging your spirit to move away from them. Surrender them to Me, and sit with Me, my beloved.

NOVEMBER 11ᵀᴴ

Finding Strength in the Storm

> Psalm 139:2

You know, when I sit, and when I rise, you perceive my thoughts from afar.

> Malachi 3:10

Bring the whole tithe into the storehouse, that there may be food in my house. Test me in this," says the Lord Almighty, "and see if I will not throw open the floodgates of heaven and pour out so much blessing that there will not be room enough to store it.

The Father is saying, "Even in the midst of the storm, I am faithful. I will give you strength when you are weak, for you find true strength in your weakness." The battle is not yours; it is Mine, says the Lord. Trust that even the smallest detail is in My hands when things occur, and you do not understand why. I know what is best for you. I am the Lord your God; I know when you sit down and when you rise up.

Praise and worship Me through it all. Test My faithfulness, says the Lord Almighty, and see if I will not open the floodgates of heaven and pour out so many blessings that you will not have room enough to contain them.

NOVEMBER 12ᵀᴴ

Trusting God with Every Concern

Numbers 23:19

God is not human, that he should lie, not a human being, that he should change his mind. Does he speak and then not act? Does he promise and not fulfill?

John 12:44

Then Jesus cried out, "Whoever believes in me does not believe in me only, but in the one who sent me.

The Father is saying, "Time spent with Me is always time well spent." Bring every concern you have and lay it at My feet. You can trust Me completely with your life. Release all burdens to Me, including your finances and family circumstances. It is better in My hands than in yours, my beloved. Surrender everything to Me fully.

I understand you may feel overwhelmed and uncertain about the future. Yet, you can trust that every promise I have made to you is yes and amen. God is not a man who lies or changes His mind. Has He ever spoken and failed to act? Has He ever promised and not fulfilled it? Have faith in Me alone.

NOVEMBER 13ᵀᴴ

Christ, Your Firm Foundation

Hebrews 13:8

Jesus Christ is the same yesterday and today and forever.

Jeremiah 32:27

"I am the Lord, the God of all mankind. Is anything too hard for me?

The Father is saying, "Make Christ your firm foundation. I will never let you down." People may leave and give up on you, but My love for you remains steadfast and unchanging. I am the same yesterday, today, and forever. When life feels unstable, whisper My name, and I will be there. I am the Lord, the God of all mankind. Is anything too difficult for Me? Silence all voices and distractions so you can hear My still, small voice calling you. Many of My children desire to hear Me speak, but I communicate daily through My Word and My prophets. I speak continually to you. Quiet the noise around you and rest in My presence as you seek My face.

NOVEMBER 14ᵀᴴ

Seeking the Lord's Provision

Psalm 34:10

The lions may grow weak and hungry, but those who seek the Lord lack no good thing.

James 1:4

Let perseverance finish its work so that you may be mature and complete, not lacking anything.

Psalm 37:5

Commit your way to the Lord; trust in him, and he will do this:

The Father is saying that although lions may grow weak and hungry, those who seek the Lord lack no good thing. Continue to seek Me in all your ways. If you need grace, ask Me, and I will give it freely. If you need perseverance to complete the work I assigned, ask for it. Let perseverance finish its work so you may be mature and complete, lacking nothing.

Now that you have fully surrendered to Me, everything is about to change—your family, your lost friend, and your co-worker for whom you have been praying. There is nothing too impossible for Me. The impossible becomes possible with faith and belief. Commit your way to the Lord, trust in Me, and I will act.

NOVEMBER 15ᵀᴴ

Embracing the Eternal Amidst the Temporary

John 10:18

No one takes it from me, but I lay it down of my own accord. I have authority to lay it down and authority to take it up again. This command I received from my Father."

John 5:24

"Very truly, I tell you, whoever hears my word and believes him who sent me has eternal life and will not be judged but has crossed over from death to life.

The Father is saying that what you're going through is temporary; your feelings are temporary. But I am eternal. Whoever hears My word and believes in the One who sent Me has everlasting life. Such a person will not face judgment but has passed from death to life.

Are you willing to lay everything down for My sake? Lay down that addiction, that harmful habit, or that person I have asked you to distance yourself from. Turn away from what serves no purpose in your life. No one can take My life from Me; I laid it down voluntarily and can take it up again according to My Father's command.

NOVEMBER 16ᵀᴴ

Focusing on the Heart

| Matthew 10:1

Look, I am sending you out as sheep among wolves. So be as shrewd as snakes and harmless as doves.

The Father is saying that there is no weapon too big for me to dismantle. The enemy tried everything and failed. For some of you, the enemy attempted old habits. He even tried using old habits as a temptation for you, but I hear the Lord, no weapon formed against you shall prosper in Jesus' name. Those people, places, and things don't work anymore. The enemy is frustrated because he has tried everything literally, and you keep serving me; you keep showing up, and you didn't back out when times got hard. You kept showing up, and you kept pressing to the goal. Every attack of witchcraft and every hex and every curse in Jesus' name. I am breaking it off, says the Lord. I am breaking it off at this hour. for you will know, says the Lord, I am your God. I am a big God.

There is no higher power than me. I have all the power and authority. When your enemies look at you, they will know it's only through the hand of God that upon your life, he failed the enemy; every time the enemy tried, he failed. Old tactics aren't working because I have given you wisdom to know when the enemy is lurking or when a devil is lurking. I am increasing your discernment, which is [explanation of discernment]. You have asked for it. You will know the real from the counterfeit. No more will the devil taunt you or harass you in Jesus' name.

NOVEMBER 17TH

Heart Over Appearance

> Ephesians 3:20

Now to him who is able to do immeasurably more than all we ask or imagine, according to his power that is at work within us,

The Father is saying that while you may focus on your outward appearance, I look at your heart and its posture. Do not be overly concerned with your external appearance or weight. Instead, make healthier food choices and ask My Holy Spirit to guide you. The Holy Spirit, your advocate, will support you in all things. Trust that I can do all things in your life. I am Almighty God, El Shaddai. As you serve Me, you will receive anything you ask in My name, in Jesus' name. Above all, guard your heart, for everything you do flows from it.

NOVEMBER 18TH

God of Breakthrough

> Romans 8:31

What, then, shall we say in response to these things? If God is for us, who can be against us?

> 2 Samuel 5:20

So David went to Baal Perazim, and there he defeated them. He said, "As waters break out, the Lord has broken out against my enemies before me." So, that place was called Baal Perazim.[a]

> 1 Chronicles 14:11

So David and his men went up to Baal Perazim, and there he defeated them. He said, "As waters break out, God has broken out against my enemies by my hand." So, that place was called Baal Perazim.

The Father is saying, "I am the God of breakthrough." You are on the brink of overcoming that addiction, curse, or financial difficulty that has troubled you. In the name of Jesus, I will guide you through it. Something is stirring—it's on the verge of shattering! It will break through because the blood of Jesus stands against every disease and curse.

When I say I am preparing to bring you out, I am equipping you to break free from every generational curse, financial issue, and form of bondage. These burdens are about to be lifted from you in the mighty name of Jesus. Remember, you are Mine. If I am for you, who can stand against you? No one.

NOVEMBER 19ᵀᴴ

The Shepherd's Unfailing Love

Luke 15:4

"Suppose one of you has a hundred sheep and loses one of them. Doesn't he leave the ninety-nine in the open country and go after the lost sheep until he finds it?

Exodus 14:14

The Lord will fight for you; you need only to be still."

Revelation 1:18

I am the Living One; I was dead, and now look, I am alive forever and ever! And I hold the keys of death and Hades.

The Father is saying, "I would leave the ninety-nine just for you, my one lost sheep." Just as a man with a hundred sheep will leave the ninety-nine on the mountain to search for the lost one, I passionately pursue you. I would chase you down and fight for you.

I died and rose again, and I am alive forevermore. Amen. I hold the keys of Hades and Death. No demon, warlock, or force can separate you from My love. I will always stand up for you and fight for you. You are Mine, and I am yours. Remember, you are cherished and important to Me, always.

NOVEMBER 20ᵀᴴ

The Promise of Return

Matthew 21:29-31

²⁹ "'I will not,' he answered, but later he changed his mind and went. ³⁰ "Then the father went to the other son and said the same thing. He answered, 'I will, sir,' but he did not go. ³¹ "Which of the two did what his father wanted?" "The first," they answered. Jesus said to them, "Truly I tell you, the tax collectors and the prostitutes are entering the kingdom of God ahead of you.

Luke 15:11-32

Jesus continued: "There was a man who had two sons. ¹² The younger one said to his father, 'Father, give me my share of the estate.' So he divided his property between them. ¹³ "Not long after that, the younger son got together all he had, set off for a distant country, and there squandered his wealth in wild living. ¹⁴ After he had spent everything, there was a severe famine in that whole country, and he began to be in need. ¹⁵ So he went and hired himself out to a citizen of that country, who sent him to his fields to feed pigs. ¹⁶ He longed to fill his stomach with the pods that the pigs were eating, but no one gave him anything. ¹⁷ "When he came to his senses, he said, 'How many of my father's hired servants have food to spare, and here I am starving to death! ¹⁸ I will set out and go back to my father and say to him: Father, I have sinned against heaven and against you. ¹⁹ I am no longer worthy to be called your son; make me like one of your hired servants.' ²⁰ So he got up and went to his father. "But while he was still a long way off, his father saw him and was filled with compassion for him; he ran to his son, threw his arms around him and kissed him. ²¹

"The son said to him, 'Father, I have sinned against heaven and against you. I am no longer worthy to be called your son.'[22] "But the father said to his servants, 'Quick! Bring the best robe and put it on him. Put a ring on his finger and sandals on his feet.[23] Bring the fattened calf and kill it. Let's have a feast and celebrate. [24] For this son of mine was dead and is alive again; he was lost and is found.' So they began to celebrate. [25] "Meanwhile, the older son was in the field. When he came near the house, he heard music and dancing. [26] So he called one of the servants and asked him what was going on. [27] 'Your brother has come,' he replied, 'and your father has killed the fattened calf because he has him back safe and sound.' [28] "The older brother became angry and refused to go in. So his father went out and pleaded with him. [29] But he answered his father, 'Look! All these years I've been slaving for you and never disobeyed your orders. Yet you never gave me even a young goat so I could celebrate with my friends. [30] But when this son of yours who has squandered your property with prostitutes comes home, you kill the fattened calf for him!' [31] "'My son,' the father said, 'you are always with me, and everything I have is yours. [32] But we had to celebrate and be glad, because this brother of yours was dead and is alive again; he was lost and is found.'"

NOVEMBER 21ST

Obeying the Still Small Voice

> Matthew 8:27

The men were amazed and asked, "What kind of man is this? Even the winds and the waves obey him!"

> John 10:27

My sheep listen to my voice; I know them, and they follow me.

The Father is saying, "Obey every command I have given you." It is crucial to listen to My still, small voice. When I speak, everything moves; mountains shift, and storms cease. Remember how the disciples were terrified and asked, "Who is this man? Even the wind and the waves obey Him!"

Do not have little faith or be afraid, beloved. I am the God who rebukes the winds and the sea and calms the storm perfectly. Do not entertain unbelief or doubt in what I do or say. Rebuke every voice that is not of Me. My sheep hear My voice; I know them, and they follow Me.

NOVEMBER 22ᴺᴰ

Resting in the God of Restoration

Exodus 3:6

Then he said, "I am the God of your father,[a] the God of Abraham, the God of Isaac, and the God of Jacob." At this, Moses hid his face because he was afraid to look at God.

Genesis 50:20

You intended to harm me, but God intended it for good to accomplish what is now being done: the saving of many lives.

The Father is saying, "Oh, you of little faith, remember that I am the God who sits on the throne. Cast aside all unbelief, for I, the Lord, provide everything you need." I am working behind the scenes for you and your family every moment. I am the God who restores dead things and brings everything into order.

I am your God, the God of Abraham, Isaac, and Jacob. Have faith in Me alone. While the enemy may intend to harm you, I turn it all for good. Therefore, thank and worship Me, knowing I am in control and working for your benefit.

NOVEMBER 23RD

Worshiping Through Trials

Matthew 6:25-34

"Therefore, I tell you, do not worry about your life, what you will eat or drink, or about your body, what you will wear. Is not life more than food and the body more than clothes? ²⁶ Look at the birds of the air; they do not sow or reap or store away in barns, and yet your heavenly Father feeds them. Are you not much more valuable than they? ²⁷ Can any one of you, by worrying, add a single hour to your life? ²⁸ "And why do you worry about clothes? See how the flowers of the field grow. They do not labor or spin. ²⁹ Yet I tell you that not even Solomon in all his splendor was dressed like one of these.³⁰ If that is how God clothes the grass of the field, which is here today and tomorrow is thrown into the fire, will he not much more clothe you—you of little faith? ³¹ So do not worry, saying, 'What shall we eat?' or 'What shall we drink?' or 'What shall we wear?'³² For the pagans run after all these things, and your heavenly Father knows that you need them. ³³ But seek first his kingdom and his righteousness, and all these things will be given to you as well. ³⁴ Therefore, do not worry about tomorrow, for tomorrow will worry about itself. Each day has enough trouble of its own.

The Father is saying, "When you face any trial or tribulation, worship Me with thanksgiving." Acknowledge My sovereignty and goodness even amidst difficulties. Thank Me for the problem, the trial, the storm, or the testing. I, your Father, fill you with My presence and grant you peace. The peace I give is not like the world's peace. Do not let your hearts be troubled or afraid. I am always with you. Instead of worrying, pray about every issue and circumstance, even those things or people you might feel embarrassed to mention. Bring everything to Me, and I will guide and lead you.

NOVEMBER 24ᵀᴴ

Satisfied by Righteousness

Matthew 5:6

Blessed are those who hunger and thirst for righteousness, for they will be filled.

Mark 9:2-3

After six days, Jesus took Peter, James, and John with him and led them up a high mountain, where they were all alone. There, he was transfigured before them. ³ His clothes became dazzling white, whiter than anyone in the world could bleach them.

The Father is saying, "Blessed are those who hunger and thirst for righteousness, for they shall be satisfied." It is a blessing that you desire to live according to My will. Ask the Holy Spirit to provide what you need today, and thank Me for every thing. I am the reason for your transformation and the source of your strength. Remember, I am always with you through every step of your journey. Commune with me always, and do not hesitate to contact your father with your requests. I am here, listening to every word you pray.

NOVEMBER 25TH

One Father in Heaven

Matthew 23:9

And do not call anyone on earth 'father,' for you have one Father, and he is in heaven.

John 14:12

Very truly, I tell you, whoever believes in me will do the works I have been doing, and they will do even greater things than these because I am going to the Father.

The Father is saying, "Do not call anyone on earth Father, for you have one Father, and He is in heaven." He provides for all your needs, giving you what you require at the perfect time. He is unchanging, the same yesterday, today, and forever. He knows your longing to see Him, and you will. Continue seeking His face and following His will.

Ask the Holy Spirit to guide and lead you and to fill your life with love. He will give you eyes to see and ears to hear. As you look at others, you will see them through His eyes and hear what the Spirit is saying. He always speaks through His word, people, songs, and nature. His voice is ever-present.

NOVEMBER 26TH

Faith Makes All Things Possible

Matthew 19:26

Jesus looked at them and said, "With man, this is impossible, but with God, all things are possible."

2 Corinthians 2:14

But thanks be to God, who always leads us as captives in Christ's triumphal procession and uses us to spread the aroma of the knowledge of him everywhere.

The Father is saying, "Anything is possible if you believe." With Me, all things are possible! What may seem impossible for men is achievable with God. Those who have faith in Me and believe with their whole heart understand that nothing is too hard. Ask the Holy Spirit to remove all doubt and strengthen your faith in Jesus' name.

Let us thank God, who always leads us as captives in Christ's triumphal procession and uses us to spread the fragrance of the knowledge of Him everywhere.

NOVEMBER 27ᵀᴴ

Pray Boldly

Luke 18:27

Jesus replied, "What is impossible with man is possible with God."

Hebrews 10:35-36

So do not throw away your confidence; it will be richly rewarded. ³⁶ You need to persevere so that when you have done the will of God, you will receive what he has promised.

The Father is saying that you should start the day by praying boldly. Remember, you serve a mighty God, and nothing is too big for Him. If He is for you, no one can be against you. So, begin today with bold prayers, understanding that if you lack something, it is because you haven't asked. You have not because you ask not.

Approach Him confidently, knowing you serve an all-powerful God, your Father, on earth and in heaven. Have faith and believe that anything is possible. What is impossible with men is possible with God. He will answer every prayer prayed with faith and belief. Trust in Him alone, for nothing is too hard for Him, says the Lord.

NOVEMBER 28ᵀᴴ

Understanding Your Identity in Christ

Ephesians 2:6

And God raised us up with Christ and seated us with him in the heavenly realms in Christ Jesus,

Luke 10:19

I have given you authority to trample on snakes and scorpions and to overcome all the power of the enemy; nothing will harm you.

The Father is saying, "Understand your identity and belonging in Christ Jesus." You are not merely a believer; you are My beloved child, and I am your Father. Remember, God raised us with Christ and seated us in the heavenly realms.

Pray with conviction, asking for confusion to be sent into the enemy's camp and commanding that every blessing stolen by the enemy be returned to you in Jesus' name. You have been given power and authority over all the enemy's power. Do not fear anything. Know that I am your Lord, your God, and will strengthen you in every season and battle. You are not just a conqueror; you are victorious in Christ Jesus. You are not just a survivor but an overcomer in Jesus' name.

NOVEMBER 29ᵀᴴ

Guided by My Spirit

Zechariah 4:6

So he said to me, "This is the word of the Lord to Zerubbabel: 'Not by might nor by power, but by my Spirit,' says the Lord Almighty.

Matthew 6:33

But seek first his kingdom and his righteousness, and all these things will be given to you as well.

The Father is saying, "Not by might nor by power, but by My Spirit." You have been made new and whole. It is by My Spirit that each step you take is guided, and it is by My Spirit that you will be taught My ways and have your mind renewed.

Although you will face hardships, persecutions, trials, and tribulations, My Spirit will see you through them all. I am the one who directs the steps of the righteous and restores order to what is out of place. Seek the Kingdom of God and His righteousness first, and all these things will be given to you. It is by My Spirit that everything you need is provided.

NOVEMBER 30ᵀᴴ

The True Treasure

Isaiah 45:3

I will give you hidden treasures, riches stored in secret places,

so that you may know that I am the Lord, the God of Israel, who summons you by name.

Matthew 6:20

But store up for yourselves treasures in heaven, where moths and vermin do not destroy, and where thieves do not break in and steal.

The Father is saying that the treasure you're seeking is found in Me. I will give you the treasures hidden in darkness and the wealth stored in secret places so you may know that I, the Lord, the God of Israel, call you by name. While you search for treasures in this world, remember that true wealth is not found here. The Lord says the silver and gold are Mine; they are not creations of man but are made valuable by My design.

Gold and silver are intrinsically valuable and beautiful products of Me. They do not tarnish or corrode. Therefore, I urge you to store your treasures in heaven, where moths and vermin cannot destroy. These heavenly treasures represent the spiritual rewards and blessings that far surpass earthly riches. I am the Lord who gives and takes away. I am your God.

DECEMBER 1ST

Covered and Protected

Luke 12:7

Indeed, the very hairs of your head are all numbered. Don't be afraid; you are worth more than many sparrows.

Psalm 91:4

He will cover you with his feathers, and under his wings, you will find refuge; his faithfulness will be your shield and rampart.

Matthew 10:29

Are not two sparrows sold for a penny? Yet not one of them will fall to the ground outside your Father's care.

The Father is saying, "I know the number of hairs on your head; you are worth more than many sparrows. I know you intimately, like the back of My hand." Do not fear anything; I am with you from sunrise to sunset. I hide under My wing and cover you with My feathers; you will find refuge under My wings. My faithfulness will be your shield and rampart.

When you feel afraid, whisper My precious name, Jesus, and I will be there. Are not two sparrows sold for a penny? Yet not one of them falls to the ground without My knowledge. I know when you rise and will always watch over you.

DECEMBER 2ND

Running the Race with Endurance

Isaiah 41:13

For I am the Lord your God who takes hold of your right hand and says to you, Do not fear; I will help you.

Hebrews 12:1-7

Therefore, since we are surrounded by such a great cloud of witnesses, let us throw off everything that hinders and the sin that so easily entangles. And let us run with perseverance the race marked out for us, ² fixing our eyes on Jesus, the pioneer and perfecter of faith. For the joy set before him, he endured the cross, scorning its shame, and sat down at the right hand of the throne of God. ³ Consider him who endured such opposition from sinners, so that you will not grow weary and lose heart.⁴ In your struggle against sin, you have not yet resisted to the point of shedding your blood. ⁵ And have you completely forgotten this word of encouragement that addresses you as a father addresses his son? It says, "My son, do not make light of the Lord's discipline, and do not lose heart when he rebukes you,⁶ because the Lord disciplines the one he loves, and he chastens everyone he accepts as his son."⁷ Endure hardship as discipline; God is treating you as his children. For what children are not disciplined by their father?

The Father is saying, "I am your God, the Lord who holds your hand." Do not be afraid, for I am here to help you. I will strengthen you and provide the endurance you need as you run the race set before you. Ask the Holy Spirit to increase your endurance.

Look to Jesus, the founder, and perfecter of your faith, who, for the joy set before Him, endured the cross, despising its shame, and is now seated at the right hand of the throne of God. You will face trials, tribulations, and tests, but rejoice and be glad, for you are suffering for My name."

DECEMBER 3ʳᵈ

The Light of Holiness

1 Peter 1:16

for it is written: "Be holy because I am holy."

1 Timothy 6:15

which God will bring about in his own time—God, the blessed and only Ruler, the King of kings and Lord of Lords,

The Father is saying, "Where I am, darkness cannot remain. I am holy, and it is written, Be holy because I am holy." This call to holiness is so you may live a righteous, pure, and sanctified life. If you need assistance in any area of your life, ask My Holy Spirit. He is here to extend grace and bring new life to those areas.

I am the King of Kings, the Lord of Lords, the great, mighty, and awesome God, who is impartial and takes no bribe. I renew, rejuvenate, and restore you, making all things new. The past is gone, and the new has come in Jesus' name. Do everything to glorify My name, the name above every name. Worship Me with songs of thanksgiving."

DECEMBER 4ᵀᴴ

Coming to God with Your Whole Self

Exodus 14:15

Then the Lord said to Moses, "Why are you crying out to me? Tell the Israelites to move on.

Matthew 24:6

You will hear of wars and rumors of wars, but see to it that you are not alarmed. Such things must happen, but the end is still to come.

The Father is saying, "You don't need to be perfect to come to Me." Bring your scars, wounds, and brokenness; I can heal every part of you. You've endured trauma and taken hard hits, but rise and keep fighting. Remember who is with you—I am with you. I will fight every battle; you need only to be still. No valley is too deep or mountain too high for Me to move.

I am the God of Abraham, Isaac, and Jacob. Do not be alarmed by the presence of the enemy or dismayed by troubling news. You will hear of wars and rumors of wars but do not be shaken. Such things must occur, but the end is still to come. Trust in Me, your God, and find strength and peace in My presence."

DECEMBER 5ᵀᴴ

Rising Again with Strength

Ecclesiastes 4:12

Though one may be overpowered, two can defend themselves.

A cord of three strands is not quickly broken.

2 Timothy 1:7

For the Spirit God gave us does not make us timid but gives us power, love, and self-discipline.

The Father is saying that although the righteous may fall seven times, they rise again, while the wicked stumble in times of trouble. Life's journey is filled with highs and lows, but you have the strength to rise each time you fall. Though people, places, and circumstances may change, I remain unchanging.

When fear begins to creep in, bind it with the strength of a three-stranded cord in the mighty name of Jesus. Even if you feel overwhelmed, remember that while two can defend themselves, a cord of three strands is not easily broken. I have not given you a spirit of fear but one of power, love, and a sound mind. Maintain hope in every situation, knowing that I am moving on your behalf in all you do.

DECEMBER 6ᵀᴴ

Conquer Through His Love

Romans 8:37-39

No, in all these things we are more than conquerors through him who loved us. ³⁸ For I am convinced that neither death nor life, neither angels nor demons, neither the present nor the future, nor any powers, ³⁹ neither height nor depth, nor anything else in all creation, will be able to separate us from the love of God that is in Christ Jesus our Lord.

Romans 8:28'

And we know that in all things God works for the good of those who love him, who have been called according to his purpose.

The Father is saying, "Through Him, you can conquer anything. You are more than a conqueror through Him who loves you in all these things. Nothing—neither death nor life, angels nor rulers, present nor future, powers, height, depth, nor anything else in all creation—can separate you from the love of God in Christ Jesus our Lord."

Do not be swayed by the enemy's deceit; he is the father of lies. Seek the Holy Spirit for spiritual discernment and place your trust solely in me. I will never leave you nor forsake you. As your Father, I am working all things together for the good of those in Christ Jesus. Reject distractions, trust in my plan, and you will discover hope and purpose.

DECEMBER 7ᵀᴴ

Emerging Victorious

2 Corinthians 10:4

The weapons we fight with are not the weapons of the world. On the contrary, they have divine power to demolish strongholds.

Psalm 21:11

Though they plot evil against you and devise wicked schemes, they cannot succeed.

The Father is saying that many of you are emerging from a season of intense warfare. It may have felt like an endless uphill battle, but the war has been won. I have been with you through every moment, guiding and supporting you. Speak the promises of God into your current situation and watch as I move on your behalf. Remember, transformation occurs not by might or power but by the Spirit of the living God.

This battle and the circumstances surrounding it are shifting for the better. I tested your faith to strengthen you, but you have always been aware of My presence. You are now preparing for a new season, a new level, and a new dimension of growth. I am so proud of you for standing firm against attacks and for using the armor of God to defend yourself.

By faith, we stand together and rebuke every plot and scheme of the enemy. You are a warrior in the spiritual realm, equipped and ready for what comes next.

DECEMBER 8TH

Embracing Your Royal Identity

> 2 Kings 3:16

and he said, "This is what the Lord says: I will fill this valley with pools of water.

> Ephesians 3:20-21

Now to him who is able to do immeasurably more than all we ask or imagine, according to his power that is at work within us, [21] to him be glory in the church and in Christ Jesus throughout all generations, forever and ever! Amen.

The Father is saying, "Fix your crown, my child. You are a daughter or a son of a King! Know who you belong to in Jesus' name." The Lord declares, "I will make this dry streambed full of pools." In moments of weakness, ask my Holy Spirit to fill you. When you are unsure of what to pray, the Holy Spirit will intercede with groanings too deep for words. He will guide and lead you in ways you do not expect. Anticipate the unexpected, for I am the God who surpasses your imagination. I am always with you. Focus your full attention on Me, says the Lord. Bind every distraction and rebuke every attack on your mind, family, marriage, and ministry. The blood of Jesus covers everything in Jesus' name.

DECEMBER 9TH

Chosen and Appointed

Deuteronomy 14:2

for you are a people holy to the Lord your God. Out of all the peoples on the face of the earth, the Lord has chosen you to be his treasured possession.

Numbers 23:19

¹⁹ God is not human, that he should lie, not a human being, that he should change his mind. Does he speak and then not act? Does he promise and not fulfill?

The Father is saying that you have been set apart as holy to the Lord your God. He has chosen you from all the nations of the earth to be His special treasure. You are called and appointed for a time such as this. If you have been seeking confirmation, here it is: I have called and qualified you. What your enemies say doesn't matter; what I, the Lord, have spoken will come to pass in Jesus' name. Remember, God is not a man, that He should lie, or a son of man, that He should change His mind. Has He said, and will He not do it? Or has He spoken, and will He not fulfill it? Rejoice, for God is actively fighting for you and moving on your behalf in Jesus' name.

DECEMBER 10ᵀᴴ

Renew Your Mind and Heart

> Ephesians 4:31

Get rid of all bitterness, rage and anger, brawling and slander, along with every form of malice.

The Father is saying to let go of all harmful mindsets. Replace all stinking thinking with a request for His Holy Spirit to dismantle every demonic influence and renew your mind. Seek the Holy Spirit's guidance to cleanse your heart of unrighteousness, removing bitterness, rage, anger, brawling, slander, and all forms of malice. These evil things are not of Him but of the enemy, and they need to be burned away with the fire of the Holy Spirit in Jesus' name. Instead, embrace the fruit of the Spirit—love, joy, peace, patience, kindness, generosity, faithfulness, gentleness, and self-control. By doing so, you will experience personal growth, and the Holy Spirit will help you bear much fruit in Jesus' name.

DECEMBER 11TH

Complete Trust in the Father

Proverbs 3:5

Trust in the Lord with all your heart and lean not on your own understanding.

The Father is saying, "Trust Me with all of your heart, mind, and soul." There is no room for hesitation. I understand your struggle with trusting Me, so I urge you to trust Me completely and not rely on your understanding. In all your ways, submit to Me, and I will make your paths straight. It is time to place your trust in Me regarding that job, the child who is lost to addiction, the troubled marriage, or the relationship that seems hopeless. There is hope for every situation. Be still and trust Me with all your heart, mind, and soul. It is time for less talk and more action for My kingdom. Remember, without faith, it is impossible to please Me. Anyone who comes to Me must believe I exist and reward those who earnestly seek Me.

DECEMBER 12ᵀᴴ

Trusting While Waiting

John 16:33

"I have told you these things so that in me you may have peace. In this world, you will have trouble. But take heart! I have overcome the world."

Romans 8:37

No, in all these things, we are more than conquerors through him who loved us.

1 John 4:4

You, dear children, are from God and have overcome them because the one who is in you is greater than the one who is in the world.

The Father is saying, "Lean into My presence as you wait for Me." Waiting on Me is an act of trust. I delight in seeing My children trust Me wholeheartedly and depend on nothing and no one but Me. I have nothing to do with idols or worldly things. Although the enemy deceives many, you, beloved, have My Holy Spirit, and you will bear fruit in My name. You will receive whatever you ask in My name, with faith and belief that I am the one true God. With Me, all things are possible. Even faith as small as a mustard seed can move mountains. You can overcome anything with Me—whether it's a job, success, addiction, or a hidden struggle that I alone know and see. Ask My Holy Spirit to purge everything not of Me in Jesus' name.

DECEMBER 13TH

Offering Your First Fruits

▌ Proverbs 3:9-10

Honor the Lord with your wealth, with the first fruits of all your crops; ¹⁰ then your barns will be filled to overflowing, and your vats will brim over with new wine.

▌ Malachi 3:10

Bring the whole tithe into the storehouse, that there may be food in my house. "Test me in this" says the Lord Almighty, "and see if I will not throw open the floodgates of heaven and pour out so much blessing that there will not be room enough to store it."

The Father is saying, "Bring Me your first fruits. I am your provider, Jehovah Jireh. God will provide." Honor the Lord with your wealth and the first fruits of all your produce. In doing so, your barns will be filled with plenty, and your vats will overflow with new wine. Recognize that any income you receive is a blessing from heaven. Be a cheerful giver, bringing the full tithe into the storehouse so that there may be food in My house. Test Me in this, says the Lord of hosts, and see if I will not open the windows of heaven and pour out a blessing until there is no more need. Rejoice in the promise of abundance, for it is a beacon of hope and optimism.

DECEMBER 14ᵀᴴ

Moving Forward with God

Isaiah 43:18-19

"Forget the former things; do not dwell on the past. ¹⁹ See, I am doing a new thing! Now it springs up; do you not perceive it? I am making a way in the wilderness and streams in the wasteland.

Genesis 19:26

But Lot's wife looked back, and she became a pillar of salt.

The Father is saying, "Don't look back. The enemy will use your past to prevent you from moving forward into God's good things and plans for you." Avoid being like Lot's wife, who, out of disobedience, looked back and was turned into a pillar of salt. Do not return to old ways, mindsets, or people from which God has delivered you. Forget the former things and do not dwell in the past. Instead, fix your eyes forward with God as your focus and priority. He will guide you and instruct you on the way you should go.

DECEMBER 15TH

The Ultimate Helper

> Psalm 121:1
>
> I lift up my eyes to the mountains— where does my help come from?

> Psalm 3:3
>
> But you, Lord, are a shield around me, my glory, the One who lifts my head high.

The Father is saying that He is the ultimate helper. Focus on His presence, and you will find the strength you need for any situation, issue, or circumstance. Everything you need can be found in Him. You will find fulfillment in Him if you feel any sense of lack. Every desire of your heart is met only through Him. The love and wholeness you seek are in Him. If you lack love from a parent or friend, remember that He is your Father now. He promises to love you unconditionally and never leave or forsake you. He is always here with open arms, waiting for you, His beloved. Lift up your eyes and ask where your help comes from—the Lord, the maker of heaven and earth. Indeed, the One who watches over Israel will neither slumber nor sleep. There is no other helper but the one who made us.

DECEMBER 16ᵀᴴ

Embracing New Beginnings

Malachi 3:10-11

Bring the whole tithe into the storehouse, that there may be food in my house. Test me in this," says the Lord Almighty, "and see if I will not throw open the floodgates of heaven and pour out so much blessing that there will not be room enough to store it.¹¹ I will prevent pests from devouring your crops, and the vines in your fields will not drop their fruit before it is ripe," says the Lord Almighty.

Isaiah 43:19

See, I am doing a new thing! Now it springs up; do you not perceive it? I am making a way in the wilderness and streams in the wasteland.

The Father is saying, "I am making all things new. Out with the old and in with the new. Behold, I am doing a new thing!" This could be a new job, relationship, or an opportunity you've been waiting for. Now it springs up—do you not perceive it? I am making a way in the wilderness and streams in the wasteland. I am creating a path where none seems to exist. Instead of being distracted, look up to Me, where your help comes from. I am opening doors to new opportunities, jobs, and relationships. Do you not perceive it, My beloved? I am working all things out for your good. Ask My Holy Spirit to reveal these new opportunities to you, and see if I will not open the floodgates of heaven and pour out so many blessings that you won't have room to contain them."

DECEMBER 17TH

Renewed in His Grace

2 Corinthians 12:9

But he said to me, "My grace is sufficient for you, for my power is made perfect in weakness." Therefore, I will boast all the more gladly about my weaknesses so that Christ's power may rest on me.

Malachi 3:6

"I, the Lord, do not change. So you, the descendants of Jacob, are not destroyed.

The Father is saying, "Listen, my child, do not be discouraged. I, your Father, am diligently working all things together for your good. Remember to come to repentance whenever you realize you've made a mistake." Turn back to Me, my beloved, for I am constantly working and renewing things for you. I, the Lord, do not change; therefore, you, my children, are not consumed. Change is the only constant, but I do not expect you to be perfect, as I am perfect. Seek My face, and I will fill you with My presence. Rebuke all attacks of the enemy, and he will flee from you. In Jesus' name, My grace is sufficient for you, for My power is made perfect in weakness.

DECEMBER 18TH

Guided by His Loving Eye

Psalm 32:8

I will instruct you and teach you in the way you should go; I will counsel you with my loving eye on you.

Proverbs 24:16

for though the righteous fall seven times, they rise again, but the wicked stumble when calamity strikes.

The Father is saying, "I will instruct you and teach you in the way you should go; I will counsel you with My loving eye upon you." There is no need to strive or compare your unique journey with others. The Holy Spirit, your advocate, will guide and instruct you in all your ways. Some of you have been striving and comparing your lives to others, but that is unnecessary. You are exactly where I want you to be. Even if you have stumbled, you have gotten back up and tried again. My strength is within you. Hope in Me alone, my beloved. You are perfect in My sight. A righteous person may fall seven times and rise again, but the wicked stumble in disaster and collapse.

DECEMBER 19TH

Living in His Presence

Psalm 38:8

I am feeble and utterly crushed; I groan in anguish of heart.

Psalm 95:1-7

Come, let us sing for joy to the Lord; let us shout aloud to the Rock of our salvation. ² Let us come before him with thanksgiving and extol him with music and song. ³ For the Lord is the great God, the great King above all gods. ⁴ In his hand are the depths of the earth, and the mountain peaks belong to him. ⁵ The sea is his, for he made it, and his hands formed the dry land. ⁶ Come, let us bow down in worship, let us kneel before the Lord our Maker; ⁷ for he is our God and we are the people of his pasture, the flock under his care. Today, if only you would hear his voice,

The Father is saying to be constantly aware of His presence. He is with you everywhere you go, speaking to you daily through scriptures, dreams, and even nature. He is God alone, and you will find in Him everything you need. If you ever feel like something is missing, remember that you will find it in Him. He will work out His plans for you and fulfill His purpose for your life. His steadfast love endures forever. Do not forsake the work of His hands in everything you do. Give thanks in Him, for He alone is worthy to be praised.

DECEMBER 20ᵀᴴ

Worship in Every Season

Job 1:20-21

At this, Job got up, tore his robe, and shaved his head. Then he fell to the ground in worship [21] and said: "Naked I came from my mother's womb, and naked I will depart. The Lord gave, and the Lord has taken away; may the name of the Lord be praised."

1 Corinthians 15:19

If only for this life, we have hope in Christ, we are of all people most to be pitied.

The Father is saying, "Worship Me in all things." Whether in the good or bad times, I am worthy of your praise. Do not lose sight of Me. I am faithful and unchanging. Just as Job responded in his trials by tearing his robe, shaving his head, and falling to the ground in worship, saying, "Naked I came from my mother's womb, and naked I will depart. The Lord gave, and the Lord has taken away; may the Lord's name be praised," so too should you remain steadfast. Even if you feel overwhelmed, keep your eyes on Me and trust that I will strengthen you and provide hope in every circumstance. Regardless of how things appear, I have the final say in everything and am your hope.

DECEMBER 21ST

Finding Rest in Him

1 Peter 5:7

Cast all your anxiety on him because he cares for you.

Matthew 11:28

"Come to me, all you who are weary and burdened, and I will give you rest.

The Father is saying, "I know you are facing pressures in life, marriage, and work, but remember to remain focused on Me wholeheartedly". Some of My children tend to wander and become weighed down by burdens, but these were never meant for you to carry. Cast all your anxiety on Me because I care for you. Leave everything at the feet of Jesus and let Him lift your burdens. Come to Me, all who are weary and burdened, and I will give you rest. Take My yoke upon you and learn from Me, for I am gentle and humble, and you will find rest for your souls. My yoke is easy, and My burden is light.

DECEMBER 22ND

Embracing My Plans

Isaiah 48:8

You have neither heard nor understood; from of old, your ears have not been open. Well, do I know how treacherous you are; you were called a rebel from birth.

Jeremiah 29:11

For I know the plans I have for you," declares the Lord, "plans to prosper you and not to harm you, plans to give you hope and a future.

The Father is saying, "Yes, I will reveal entirely new things to you that you have never heard before." I understand your rebellious nature, as you have been a rebel from birth. Yet, even before you were born, I knew My plans for you. You may not have always understood or considered these plans, but I have always thought about you and loved you. I know you have made mistakes, and I don't expect you to be perfect, but I ask you to trust Me and My plans for your life. For I know my plans for you, declares the Lord—plans to prosper you and not to harm you, plans to give you hope and a future.

DECEMBER 23RD

Standing on a Firm Foundation

> Romans 15:13

May the God of hope fill you with all joy and peace as you trust in him so that you may overflow with hope by the power of the Holy Spirit.

> Psalm 33:20-22

We wait in hope for the Lord; he is our help and our shield. [21] In him our hearts rejoice, for we trust in his holy name.[22] May your unfailing love be with us, Lord, even as we put our hope in you.

The Father is saying, "I am the firm foundation on which you stand. Nothing, and no one is as strong as I am. I will never fail you or forsake you." May the God of hope fill you with all joy and peace in believing so that you may overflow with hope by the power of the Holy Spirit. Trust in Me with all your heart; don't limit your trust to things or people you prefer, but place everything in My hands. They are better in Mine than anywhere else. We place our hope in the Lord. I am your protector and help. You can be glad because you trust in My holy name. May My steadfast love be with you as you continue to hope in Me."

DECEMBER 24ᵀᴴ

Trust in My Purpose

> Romans 8:28

And we know that in all things God works for the good of those who love him, who have been called according to his purpose.

> Acts 17:26

From one man, he made all the nations that they should inhabit the whole earth, and he marked out their appointed times in history and the boundaries of their lands.

The Father is saying, "We know that in all things, God works for the good of those who love Him and are called according to His purpose." Know and believe that I am God, the great I AM. Trust in Me with all your heart, mind, and soul. I am working to restore families and to free those bound by addiction. I am breaking chains of bondage in Jesus' name. Even the small concerns you have are in My hands now that you have released them to Me. I understand things may seem moving quickly, but this is My will for your life. I trust you with what I have given you and will not disappoint you.

DECEMBER 25TH

Chosen to Bear Lasting Fruit

John 15:16

You did not choose me, but I chose you and appointed you so that you might go and bear fruit—fruit that will last—and so that whatever you ask in my name, the Father will give you.

John 3:16

For God so loved the world that he gave his one and only Son, that whoever believes in him shall not perish but have eternal life.

The Father is saying, "You did not choose Me, but I chose you and appointed you to go and bear fruit—fruit that will last." Whatever you ask in My name, the Father will give you. Today is not about your gifts or money in your bank account. It's about My Son, whom I sent into the world. For God so loved the world that He gave His one and only Son, that whoever believes in Him shall not perish but have eternal life. I died so that you could be set free, delivered, and healed. That is how deeply I love you. You will know no greater love. Rejoice and be glad today and every day, for I am in you, and you are in Me.

DECEMBER 26™

Finding Joy in Trials

James 1:2-3

Consider it pure joy, my brothers and sisters, whenever you face trials of many kinds, ³ because you know that the testing of your faith produces perseverance.

Isaiah 43:2

When you pass through the waters, I will be with you, and when you pass through the rivers, they will not sweep over you.

When you walk through the fire, you will not be burned; the flames will not set you ablaze.

The Father is saying, "You will face trials; it is to be expected. Consider it pure joy, my brothers and sisters, whenever you face trials of many kinds, knowing that the testing of your faith produces perseverance." I understand that you feel overwhelmed, but that is a lie from the pit of hell. Rebuke every attack of the enemy. I will strengthen you and guide you through the fire. When you pass through the waters, I will be with you, and when you go through the rivers, they will not sweep over you. When you walk through the fire, you will not be burned; the flames will not set you ablaze.

DECEMBER 27TH

The Call to Obedience

1 Samuel 15:22

But Samuel replied: "Does the Lord delight in burnt offerings and sacrifices as much as in obeying the Lord? To obey is better than sacrifice, and to heed is better than the fat of rams.

Ephesians 4:27

and do not give the devil a foothold.

The Father is saying, "Obedience is more significant than sacrifice." If I have told you not to do something, whether through a dream or My word, heed My guidance. Some issues have arisen due to disobedience, moving you away from My will for your life. When you disobey, you open the door for the enemy. Repent and turn your heart back to Me. Ask the Holy Spirit for wisdom and grace, for My grace is sufficient. Do not dwell on your mistakes; I am a God of love and grace who forgives. Forgive yourself and move forward with Me. Samuel said, 'Has the Lord as great a delight in burnt offerings and sacrifices as in obedience to the Lord's voice? Behold, to obey is better than sacrifice, and to heed is better than the fat of rams.

DECEMBER 28ᵀᴴ

Peace in the Storm

Mark 4:39

As soon as the grain is ripe, he puts the sickle to it because the harvest has come."

Joshua 1:9

Have I not commanded you? Be strong and courageous. Do not be afraid; do not be discouraged, for the Lord your God will be with you wherever you go."

The Father is saying, "I know you are facing a storm, whether it be a sickness, a trial, or a test of your faith." Be still and know that I am God. Just as Jesus rebuked the wind and said to the sea, 'Hush, be still,' and the storm became calm, so too can you command healing for your body, restoration for your marriage, and freedom from addiction. Ask the Lord to increase your faith in every circumstance. If you are discouraged and wondering why you are going through this, remember that I am strengthening you. Have I not commanded you to be strong and courageous? Do not be afraid or discouraged, for the Lord your God is with you. This is My command: do not be afraid.

DECEMBER 29th

A Crown of Splendor

Isaiah 62:3-10

You will be a crown of splendor in the Lord's hand, a royal diadem in the hand of your God. ⁴ No longer will they call you Deserted, or name your land Desolate.But you will be called Hephzibah, and your land Beulah; for the Lord will take delight in you, and your land will be married. ⁵ As a young man marries a young woman, so will your Builder marry you; as a bridegroom rejoices over his bride, so will your God rejoice over you. I have posted watchmen on your walls, Jerusalem; they will never be silent day or night. You who call on the Lord, give yourselves no rest, ⁷ and give him no rest till he establishes Jerusalem and makes her the praise of the earth. The Lord has sworn by his right hand and by his mighty arm: "Never again will I give your grain as food for your enemies, and never again will foreigners drink the new wine for which you have toiled; ⁹ but those who harvest it will eat it and praise the Lord, and those who gather the grapes will drink it in the courts of my sanctuary." ¹⁰ Pass through, pass through the gates! Prepare the way for the people. Build up, build up the highway! Remove the stones. Raise a banner for the nations.

Malachi 3:12

"Then all the nations will call you blessed, for yours will be a delightful land," says the Lord Almighty.

The Father is saying, "You will be a crown of splendor in the Lord's hand, a royal diadem in the hand of your God." You are valuable and cherished. Some of My children feel unworthy of My love, but that is a lie from the pit of hell. Do not be swayed by temporary emotions. Instead, ask the

Holy Spirit to heal your wounds of trauma. You will be reminded of My unchanging love for you in My presence. I will never change My mind about you. Whatever you need, your Father in heaven will provide. All nations will call you blessed, for yours will be a delightful land, says the Lord Almighty.

DECEMBER 30ᵀᴴ

Honoring the Faithful

Proverbs 31:28-31

Her children arise and call her blessed; her husband also, and he praises her: ²⁹ "Many women do noble things, but you surpass them all." ³⁰ Charm is deceptive, and beauty is fleeting; but a woman who fears the Lord is to be praised. ³¹ Honor her for all that her hands have done, and let her works bring her praise at the city gate.

Exodus 14:21

Then Moses stretched out his hand over the sea, and all that night, the Lord drove the sea back with a strong east wind and turned it into dry land. The waters were divided,

The Father is saying, "Her children arise and call her blessed; her husband also praises her. Many women do noble things, but you surpass them all." Charm is deceptive, and beauty is fleeting, but a woman who fears the Lord is to be praised. Honor her for all that her hands have done, and let her works bring praise at the city gate. My beloved, I am always at work in your life, tending to every detail. There is nothing I do not know or see. I am so proud of your spiritual growth. Keep trusting in Me fully, and continue to let Me be the Lord of your life. Watch as every barrier is broken. In the name of Jesus, as you have made Me Lord over everything, I am preparing to part the Red Sea in your life.

DECEMBER 31ST

A New Year of Promise

> Jeremiah 29:11

For I know the plans I have for you," declares the Lord, "plans to prosper you and not to harm you, plans to give you hope and a future.

> Psalm 65:11

You crown the year with your bounty, and your carts overflow with abundance.

The Father is saying, "As this year comes to a close, a new year is just around the corner." It's no secret that the enemy is attacking you from every angle, trying to thwart your and My plans for you. No devil, demon, witch, or warlock can prevent the plans I have ordained for your life, declares the Lord. I know my plans for you—to prosper and not harm you, to give you hope and a future. Do not let the enemy deceive you into giving up your blessing. Many of My children forfeit their blessings by becoming discouraged when results don't come immediately. Remember, this is a process and a journey. Embrace all that I have for you in the new year. I crown this year with goodness, and your paths will overflow with abundance."

About the Author

My name is Allison Velazquez. I'm a disciple of Jesus Christ of Nazareth. I love the Lord with all my heart, mind, and soul. Jesus saved my life. Growing up as a child was never easy; I went through a lot and faced many hardships. I know that without God, I am nothing. God saved me from myself. The Lord has saved me from depression, suicide, and fear. In 2021, God gave me a vision to start a podcast. I'm on all platforms: Facebook, Instagram, YouTube, and TikTok. A few months later, He began to show me visions of writing a 365-day prophetic devotional. Whatever you may be facing, know that you will never face it alone. You have a heavenly Father who loves you and is always with you. May the Lord bless you and use you, in Jesus' name.

www.ingramcontent.com/pod-product-compliance
Lightning Source LLC
Chambersburg PA
CBHW060104170426
43198CB00010B/763